D0239683

MOREOVER

MOREOVER

Miles Kington

Robson Books

The author would like to thank The Times *for permission to reproduce material which first appeared there.*

FIRST PUBLISHED IN GREAT BRITAIN IN 1982 BY
ROBSON BOOKS LTD., BOLSOVER HOUSE, 5-6
CLIPSTONE STREET, LONDON W1P 7EB
COPYRIGHT © 1982 MILES KINGTON

British Library Cataloguing in Publication Data

Kington, Miles
  Moreover
  I. Title
  828′.91407   PR6061.I/

  ISBN 0-86051-173-1

Designed by Stonecastle Graphics

Printed in Hungary

MOREOVER – INTRODUCTION

As a humorist, it has always been my dream to write a column on the Obituary page of a newspaper, rather as it is every clown's ambition to stand behind Hamlet and make funny faces. *The Times* being the only paper with an Obituary page, this has rather limited my outlets. I have in fact been writing fairly regularly for *The Times* since the mid-1960s, for a long time as jazz reviewer, then more briefly as a television reviewer, but it was only when Harold Evans took over as editor in early 1981 that I thought I had a chance of writing humour for *The Times*.

I wrote to him outlining the sort of stuff I'd like to write.

He wrote back saying Maybe one day.

I suddenly realized that outlines are no good. You've got to provide the real thing. So every day for a week I sent him a piece as an example of the sort of thing I wanted to do, and after a week (I was actually prepared to go on for ever) he wrote back and asked me to do it in the paper. To this day I don't know whether it was just a way of getting me to stop sending him things, or whether he was just amazed at the sight of a journalist doing something for nothing and wanted me to desist before the unions got to hear of it.

When he said he had made space on the Obituary page for a daily piece, I told him I wanted to call my column Over My Dead Body. He didn't think it was a good idea. I gave him a list of about 100 titles. He told me to stop bothering him and take it up with Tony Holden, the Features Editor. Tony said he didn't like any of the ideas and what about Moreover? I thought it was lousy. Thus began a relationship of mutual honesty which carried us through for a year.

Suddenly one day (you probably read it about in all the papers, except *The Times*) Harold Evans and Tony Holden were gone, and I was still there, which I think goes to show the advantages of working on the Obituary page, or keeping a low profile, or lying at the bottom of the trenches with your hands over your ears, however you like to describe it. At the time of writing (3 pm, April 29, 1982) I am still writing daily for *The Times* and enjoying it more than anything I've ever done. People occasionally commiserate with what they think must be an immense burden. All I can say is that writing a daily piece seems easier than writing a weekly piece, as I used to for *Punch*; something to do with keeping the muscles warm and the juices flowing, I expect. They never believe me.

I would like to express my inexpressible gratitude to Harry Evans for hiring me, to Tony Holden for keeping me going and to

Charles Douglas-Hume for not firing me. Also to Oscar Turnill who went through my copy with a tooth-comb, which is certainly better than using a comb without teeth, and to all those obituary writers who do the really hard work.

I sometimes wonder if they ever dream of writing their obituaries in a humorous magazine.

Miles Kington

3.15 pm the same day

PREFACE

by Miles Kington

This preface is for all those readers who can't be bothered with long introductions.

All I want to say, really, is that this book is meant to be funny, so if you have just found it on the Literature or English Grammar shelves of the bookshop you are in, I'd be grateful if you could replace it in the Humour section. Or New Books would do fine.

Thanks.

MANY OTHERWISE perfectly normal people find that they are not naturally left or right, and have a strong urge to vote for a party in the middle. Doctors say that this is quite natural and certainly nothing to be ashamed of. But confusion and depression may be caused by not knowing whether you are a Liberal or SDP person, so I have devised a little test to establish your identity firmly:

☐ Which attitude is most nearly yours? (a) I intend to vote Social Democrat because the SDP has people like Bill Rodgers, Shirley Williams, Dr Owen and Roy Jenkins (b) I intend to vote Liberal because the SDP has people like Bill Rodgers, Shirley Williams, Dr Owen and Roy Jenkins.

☐ What was the name of David Owen's recent book? (a) I'm Getting My Act Together and Putting it on the Road (b) Warrington DC (c) Slim Along with Dr David Owen (d) Before I Answer That Question, May I Just Say This?

☐ You overhear someone say: 'I'd always thought of him as young but on the TV last night he suddenly looked old.' Do you immediately think of (a) Tony Benn (b) David [Steel] (c) Prince Charles (d) David [Owen] (e) Cliff Richard (f) yourself?

☐ You are disgusted by the way British politics never gets beyond sordid party manoeuvring. You think the best way to combat this is (a) to create a brand new party (b) no, hold on, that could only make things worse (c) as if things *could* be any worse (d) well, at least the SDP has never had a sex scandal in its history.

☐ What was your reaction when you heard that Tom Ellis, MP for Wrexham, had left Labour to join the SDP? (a) Where? (b) I'm not surprised, the way they've played this season (c) Ellis? Owen? Jenkins? Williams? But I only left the Labour Party because it had too damn many Welshmen in it . . .

☐ When you see a photo of the Gang of Four in the paper, what do you think? (a) It's nice to see at least one national executive looking united (b) I'd always thought of Roy Jenkins as old, but he's suddenly looking quite young (c) It's *Beyond the Fringe* all over again—a doctor with three supporting comics.

☐ You are watching an old movie on TV. The girl is in the arms of a young man. Suddenly James Cagney bursts in waving a gun and asks her to move to one side so he can shoot the young man (probably because he has left Cagney's gang to start a new moderate, centre gang). In your fantasy life, what would you do to

7

rescue him? (a) Jump through a window firing off Britain's nuclear deterrent (b) Crash through the skylight waving last October's party conference decision against shooting (c) Walk through the door saying: 'I am Shirley Williams and this is too ridiculous for words.'

Results: If you assume you've got maximum points, you are a Tory. If you assume you have the same points as the majority, you are Labour. If you think the point-scoring system is bound to be unfair to you, you are Liberal. If you are not sure what you think, you are SDP.

PAUL FOOT has recently shown us in his book *Red Shelley* that Shelley was not merely a lyric poet; he was also a passionate left-wing reformer, advocate of state control and anti-Marketeer. But in my forthcoming book *Red Ed* (Furious Press, £8.99½) I aim to restore the reputation of a political thinker even more neglected than Shelley: Edward Lear.

Misrepresented all these years as a writer of nonsense for children, Lear displayed an indignation and rage at Victorian injustice which makes Shelley look like a *Nationwide* reporter. Lear's poems are not silly stories; they are agonized case-histories. There was an old man of Cape Horn, fumed Lear, who wished he had never been born. Was help forthcoming? Was there adequate social care in this part of the Third World? No—he sat on a chair, till he died of despair, that dolorous man of Cape Horn. I do not recall Shelley showing equal awareness of the age trap in Latin America.

Closer to home, Lear was no less caring. There was an old person of Harrow, Lear tells us (note his pioneering use of the world 'person'), who bought a mahogany barrow, for he said to his wife You're the joy of my life and I'll wheel you all day in this barrow. That tells us all we need to know about the marriage trap—the wife treated as nothing more than a chattel, the husband, though apparently more independent, equally caught in the capitalist marriage arrangement. Note, too, Lear's side-swipe at a consumerist society; the old person could easily have used a plain barrow but had been deluded by some unscrupulous mahogany salesman into an impossible hire-purchase arrangement. I have searched the annals of Harrow, by the way, for details of this disastrous marriage, but it seems never to have come to court. Perhaps Lear's choice of Harrow as a setting is a covert reference to the fact that he would have been much more miserable if he had gone there than Shelley ever was at Eton.

It may be that Lear's language is too powerful, too direct, for us to respond to. Would we respond to him better if he used today's approach and reported that there was this old person of Cape Horn, right, who suffered severely from a depression state, not helped by the disgraceful fact that he was caught in a one-chair situation? Perhaps. Yet I prefer Lear's blunt, clear, prophetic verse. Prophetic? Certainly. Who before Lear had attacked the idiotic expense of the space race? Not Shelley, for sure. Yet we find him attacking the old man of The Hague, whose ideas he slams as being excessively vague. He built a balloon with the express purpose in mind of examining the moon, that (Lear acidly sums him up) deluded old man of The Hague. Or The Haig, as we would now call him.

The one great mystery of Lear's verse is the identification of the Dong with the Luminous Nose. The simple explanation is that in the Dong/Jumbly dichotomy he was merely attacking racial prejudice, but I intend to argue at length that the Dong, that prophet crying in a wilderness, was none other than Marx himself, and the Gromboolian Plain is a simple misprint for the British Museum Reading Room.

My book will appear in time for the Christmas rush and will be lavishly illustrated with Lear's savagely satirical drawings. The price has unfortunately risen, since I started this article, to £12.95.

THE DISCOVERY of a fingernail more than seven million years old has shattered all previous theories about the origin of man. That at least is the claim of 'Cocker' Leakey, the brilliant but blunt Cockney palaeontologist who found the fingernail and has now reconstructed the remote ancestor from which it came. Early man, it seems, was neither a nomad nor a tool-user.

'Sid, as I call him,' Cocker Leakey says, 'was pretty certainly a bit of a hell-raiser. Far from being interested in agriculture or hunting, his main concern was to have a bit of a night out with the lads. Boozing, fighting, chasing girls, that was his idea of life. The great big forehead what we've reconstructed from the fingernail must have known some mighty hangovers in its time. And he was none too particular about hygiene neither, judging from what we found under the nail. He was a right goer, was Sid.'

The concept of Homo Millwallicus, as Leakey has named him

after his home team, is totally at variance with conventional theories of early man. But then, Leakey himself is not the normal run of palaeontologist.

'Look,' he says, reclining in the private bar of Whitechapel's Skull and Trowel, a favourite resort of East End prehistorians, 'your actual palaeontologist is a middle-class bloke, right? To get into palaeontology you have to have a dad in the trade or shares in the Olduvai Gorge or whatever—strewth, it's easier to become a London docker. So of *course*, they judge early man by middle-class standards. He's a jolly old nomad, don't you know? Or, he's an absolute marvel with the tools. But blimey, life isn't like that. The breakthrough that led to man's superiority over other animals wasn't learning to use tools. It was discovering how to *down* tools and walk out on the spot, right? That's where Sid is different.'

But isn't Cocker in danger of the same mistake, of applying his own social standards to early man?

'Another crack like that and you could find your skull stove in,' Cocker says jovially. 'But joking apart, I truly believe that life hasn't changed much since Sid strode the earth and duffed up Neanderthal man. When my mates round here have a night out or go supporting England, people call them primitive. Savages. Throwbacks. They don't know how right they are! But I was the first who made the connexion.'

Ex-dustman, ex-labourer, ex-totter, Cocker Leakey has probably more experience of digging and sifting than any palaeontologist alive. His ideas could, just possibly, be massively right where others are massively wrong. A lot depends, though, on where exactly Sid's fingernail was found.

'Could be anywhere,' Cocker says evasively, beckoning for another round. 'He got around, old Sid. Always being moved on when neighbours objected to the noise. And, of course, he would cross entire continents to get to away fixtures if there was fun in the offing, and then be stranded the other end. But if you're seriously interested in getting hold of bits of Sid, I can always fix it for you. Plenty more where that came from, know what I mean?'

HI, GUYS and gals! says Jimmy Savile OBE. Here are just some of the really super bargains British Rail are offering you between now and Christmas. How's about that, then?

Jobhunter Special. A half-price reduction on any trip offered to all passengers who are unemployed, able-bodied and under 30. The only condition is that the applicant must do some part-time work for the railways during the journey, such as clearing litter from carriages, asking passengers to turn off their radios and helping to get trains back on the line which may have been derailed, for instance, by passengers asked to turn off their radios.

West Country Amnesty. As it's now cheaper to come from the West Country to London than go from London, many Devon and Cornwall people are being stranded in the big city, and the West Country is being gradually depopulated. To restore the status quo, BR are making December 6 a day of amnesty, and anyone can travel free to the West. 'Blimey! Should be quite a sight,' says Jimmy Savile OBE.

Non-stop Return Ticket. Up to 100 per cent reduction is offered to any traveller prepared to reach his or her destination, then immediately get into another train going the other way and come straight back again. Ideal for landscape-spotter, transistor-radio enthusiast or person who simply want to drink all day away from English licensing laws. (This replaces the present **Platform Ticket Day-Outing** arrangement.)

PAYE Card. Did you know that if you work on a train, as many businessmen do, you can claim the heating and lighting of the carriage against tax? And claim your ticket as rental of premises? We now have an arrangement with the Inland Revenue to report any journeys bought for tax purposes. And you can pay as much as you like, to make even a short journey a whacking great tax loss. 'Don't quite follow this one,' says Jimmy Savile OBE. 'Better take your accountant with you, to be on the safe side.'

No-Bike Card. Continuing their campaign to penalize cyclists who insist on cluttering up otherwise empty luggage vans with their machines, BR is making available a No-Bike Card to those who agree to leave their bikes at home; the card entitles cyclists to travel for the normal fare.

Next-of-Kin Special. It has been pointed out that applicants for the **Centenarian Railcard** announced last month sometimes pass away before they are able to avail themselves of it. Out of compassion, BR has now extended the facility thus purchased to the next of kin. If the late lamented have willed their estate to a body such as the National Trust or the RSPCA, only *one* representative from the body can travel. Dogs and cats who benefit from wills are not included, or people who inherit portable radios.

Agent Provocateur Coach Card. Long-distance coaches are providing fierce competition for British Rail; although slower, smaller, smellier and cramped, they are, dammit, often cheaper. However, we will pay your coach fare on condition that you on the coach grumble incessantly and say how much better the train is, spreading disaffection. 'Blimey,' says Jimmy Savile OBE. 'Things must be worse than I thought.'

Equity Railcard. Microphones and loudspeakers are now used in all main line services, but many BR personnel are unwilling or too shy to announce, 'This is your guard speaking,' or 'The chief steward is now open in the middle of the train.' Equity members will receive 50 per cent reduction on journeys where they are prepared to address the public. All announcements are strictly limited to three minutes; personal appearance in costume is not necessary; and autographs may be signed in the guard's van only after the show. Auditions every Thursday at Euston.

8.47 Shenfield to Liverpool Street Heroes Award. This being the most cancelled train in railway history, season ticket-holders are eligible for a bronze medallion or a free radio on which they can receive news of other trains from Shenfield which have been cancelled.

Autograph-Hunter Special. Many celebrities travel by train, either because it's simply the best way to travel or because the BBC are paying. Some of them, alas, behave surlily when approached for autographs or enquiries as to what Barry Norman is really like, and this is bad PR for BR. To them we offer considerable reductions in return for the promise of a smile and a signature. 'Hey—what about the rest of us?' asks Jimmy Savile OBE.

Jimmy Savile OBE Card. This entitles anyone called by this name to travel free. 'This one I like,' says Jimmy Savile OBE.

PLUCKY LITTLE Linda Conquest was the toast of all Devon yesterday (writes Rene McGrit) as the Totnes girl put up a magnificent fight at Wimbledon before going out 0-6, 0-6 to Judy Gomez, the nine-year-old sensation from Florida. Linda, ranked 1,890th in the world, ran and chased and retrieved wonderfully in a match lasting over 26 minutes on Court 49, but in the end she just wasn't quite good enough, and she could find no answer to Judy's searching forehand, backhand, serve, volley, dropshot and behind-the-back double-fisted sliced passing shot. 'No complaints,' said Linda later, 'but the conditions just weren't right for me. I'm at my best in driving rain with the wind screaming down off Dartmoor and the light failing fast. And grass isn't really my favourite surface either—I much prefer a good patch of buttercups and dandelions, with the odd cowpat here and there.'

Meanwhile, in Las Vegas last night, plucky light-medium-weight Terry Cardigan just wasn't quite good enough to get the decision against the tear-away Neanderthal fighter from New Jersey, Roberto Machismo.

After holding his own at the start, Terry just had no answer to Machismo's searching biff in the face after 20 seconds and failed to beat the count. 'I really reckoned I was ahead on points,' said gallant Terry later, 'and if I could just have stayed out of trouble for the next fifteen rounds, I would have been all right. But it was not to be.'

Back home again, Bob Dilley's plucky knock of three not out in 95 minutes wasn't quite good enough to prevent the touring Australian side from chalking up a victory by an innings and 867 runs against an Eastern Counties XI. Dilley carried his bat throughout his side's second innings for those three priceless runs and this may be the performance that finally gets him into the England side, at whose door he's been knocking so long that he was beginning to wonder if there was anyone home. At a time when most English batsmen seem incapable of anything but a forward defensive prod, Bob's favourite stroke (a snick over the top of slip) may be just the tonic the national side needs.

Another British hero this morning is 59-year-old Harold Crumpit, the Wimbledon umpire who put up such a plucky fight against the American Erich Froetz, when Froetz tried to beat him to death after a disputed line call: 'I had just called his service out,' said Crumpit afterwards, 'in the utmost good faith, though you can never be quite sure when your eyesight is failing as mine is. Then Froetz just descended on me, punching me, hitting me with his racket and firing wildly with a small pocket gun. I had no alternative but to penalize him two points. After that, I must have passed out, I'm afraid.'

Finally, a small prayer for Dr Pocket-Sinclair, the statistician who has just been drafted into the England World Cup soccer squad. Manager Ron Greenwood realizes that our hopes rest mainly on statistics now, and that nothing less than about nine points from England's last two games would guarantee survival. It would also help if Hungary and Romania failed to turn up for their remaining games and were disqualified. 'Stranger things have happened,' says Pocket-Sinclair at the controls of the England computer. 'It's about 25,000 to 1 against, admittedly, but you know, statistics is a funny old game. Don't count plucky little England out yet.'

URBAN NATURALIST

ONE OF the most colourful sights in our city streets today (writes our urban naturalist, 'Bin-Liner') is the gaily bedecked police vehicle as it flashes past on the way to its business. What that business is leave one in some doubt, as no observer that I know has ever been lucky enough to see one arriving at its destination or even stop for a moment in its headlong flight.

But did you know that their siren calls vary a great deal, like birdsong? And that, like birdsong, each call seems to contain a specific message? Next time you hear a police car approaching, listen carefully to the sound it is making; if you recognize the message, it will enliven your daily routine and—who knows?—prevent your early death.

The most familiar call, of course, is the well-known dee-DOO-dee-DOO, an interval of a minor third, or what musicians call 'that maddening bit in the middle eight of "Over The Rainbow" '. Basically, it's an expression of sheer pleasure at being able to drive so fast when other vehicles have to pull into the side or crash into each other.

But naturalists now think there may also be territorial overtones in the message such as 'I am about to drive on the wrong side of the road', 'Here we go along the pavement', or 'If you think you'll be safe on that traffic island, you don't know me'. Colours most typically are orange and white.

Blue vans, on the other hand, tend in my experience to emit a sort of non-stop jangling sound, combined with a mechanical roaring produced by driving in second gear at speeds more suited to top gear. The motive here is display; any creature in the natural world not endowed with striking plumage will attempt to call attention to itself stridently by the noise it makes, even though the message underlying it is as trivial as 'My inspector is going to be late for his train home at Waterloo if you don't move aside'.

A new cry I have noticed recently is a two-note motif in which the second note is almost inaudible, as if the siren was trying to draw breath, so DEE-sigh-DEE-sigh-DEE-aaaagh. We now think that this may be a sort of mating call, attracting the attention of other police cars; certainly there are many more police cars on the road than there used to be, which suggests a heavy programme of breeding.

It may even be to attract the attention of the distantly related fire engines and ambulances. Interbreeding has never been proved, but several naturalists have recently spotted what seems to be a cross between a police car and an ambulance, usually marked Private Ambulance. If this proved to be the offspring of two different species, it would be a very exciting discovery.

The wailing siren noise which moves up and down in a constant glissando is just the noise made by the young of the species and means, 'I have been watching far too many American cop thrillers'.

Keep well clear of this one, as also of the non-stop siren combined with flashing headlights, flashing blue top-light and sometimes even in older specimens a bell; this is the warlike call of a male police car going into battle or, more commonly, just looking for an opponent. More rarely it may mean 'I am proceeding to the police repair depot, as my siren has jammed'.

'I sincerely believe that the biggest threat to Britain today comes from industrial archaeology.'

These are tough words. They are surprising words. But Lord Tredgold sincerely believes them. As he sits in his modest office on the 55th floor of Tredgold House, from where he directs the small family firm of property speculation named after him, he looks out over rows and rows of Victorian architecture. Twenty years ago they were full of warehouses, factories and depots; now they are mostly industrial museums, working steam pump houses, restored foundries, perfectly working workhouses and craftsmen's cottages. The prospect frankly frightens him.

'Frankly, the prospect frightens me. Do you realize that, every year, an area the size of Birmingham is turned into industrial museums? It becomes what I call dead property, no longer subject to the natural laws of development. Industrial cemeteries, I call them.'

Lord Tredgold was until recently plain Simon Tredgold but, saddened by his constant exclusion from the honours list, he decided this year to change his name by deed poll to the somewhat unusual first name of Lord. His record in the world of property is a proud one. More than anyone else he was responsible for beating off the wave of archaeology that threatened to ruin the face of London in the 1960s and early 1970s.

'Overnight vast areas of the City would be razed to the ground and with a sinking feeling one would know that the archaeologists were about to move in, leaving the site bare and ugly for years while they searched for gold, silver and bottle-tops. It was an enormous struggle for us to bring the site to life again. But at least you knew the plain archaeologists would move on again in a year or two. Industrial archaeologists are worse; once they have taken a building, it is gone for ever. Did you know that an area the size of Gloucestershire is turned into agricultural museums and working water mills every Bank Holiday? Frankly, I wonder where it will all end.'

Frankly, one wonders too. Recent reports that the great naval dockyard at Portsmouth may be closed only add to the gloom, as one knows in one's heart of hearts that it will soon reopen as a working maritime museum, a land-bound *HMS Belfast*, thus joining all the churches which attract more sightseers than worshippers and the stately homes which have only visitors, not residents. Occasional notes of optimism, like the preservation of the Firestone factory site for further development, are rare indeed.

'Britain is becoming one vast museum,' mourns Lord Tredgold. 'Soon visitors to Britain will find a notice at Dover saying 'This island is now open to the public'. Did you know that an area equal to the M1 is made pedestrian-only every year? Frankly, one gives up.'

Frankly, one is tempted to do likewise.

Here is the news:

A five-mile tailback from the Hogarth Roundabout formed yesterday as angry motorists jammed the roads in protest against the demotion of newsreader Kenneth Kenneth.

From his home in Borehamwood, Kenneth Kenneth said the news had come like a bolt from the blue.

A spokesman for the BBC said later that Kenneth was not being demoted, just being re-allocated a news-reading slot.

Now the news in greater detail:

A jam five miles long formed yesterday as angry motorists took to the roads in protest against the demotion of popular newsreader Kenneth Kenneth. It stretched from the Hogarth Roundabout in West London right down the M4. Over now to Paul Spinks at the Hogarth Roundabout.

'This. Is the Hogarth Roundabout. Now. It's a quiet place, much like any other roundabout in London. But. Two hours ago. It was a seething cauldron of motorists. Unbelievable. Disgraceful. Scandalous. These were just some of the words they used when asked to comment. For they had just heard that Kenneth Kenneth, their favourite newsreader, was to be shifted from the evening news slot to the schools-only morning newscast.

'It was a scene that Hogarth himself might have relished. The eighteenth-century artist of crowd scenes and the fall of the mighty, after whom the roundabout, of course, is named, would surely have, um, relished the scene. Paul Spinks. Hogarth Roundabout.'

That was Paul Spinks, at the Hogarth Roundabout. More from him later.

Meanwhile, a BBC spokesman said that no demotion was involved in Kenneth's move. It was simply a reallocation of time slots, which was quite normal practice. Here's Dominick Dominick, our Time Slots Reallocation correspondent.

'This sort of reallocation of time slots is actually quite normal at the BBC and there may be no demotion actually involved at all. It is done quite often. For all sorts of reasons. But to outsiders it is bound to look like demotion, and there may well be widespread protests, of the kind we've seen at the Hogarth Roundabout.'

Dominick Dominick. Now, a comment from Kenneth Kenneth himself, to whom the news came as a bolt from the blue.

'Yes, the news came as a bolt from the blue, I commented today from my home in Borehamwood. Now, that comment in more detail. The news of the Hogarth Roundabout demonstration came as a bolt from the blue for me, as I had hoped to slip away from the evening news slot to the schools newscast quite unnoticed. The change was, of course, at my own request. I simply could not stand the strain of reading the same bit of news over and over again. At least with schools, they trust them to take it in first time. I can't wait to switch over. Kenneth Kenneth. My home. Borehamwood.'

Kenneth Kenneth. And now the main points of the news again. A five-mile tailback from the Hogarth Roundabout...

17

URBAN NATURALIST

THE WARM air hand drier is a native of the United States (urban naturalist 'Bin-Liner' writes) but it has been introduced recently to Britain and spread so rapidly that it threatens to oust the friendly British roller towel, just as the grey squirrel once decimated the red squirrel. Hardly a motorway service area, office washroom, hotel gentlemen's lavatory or (for all I know) ladies' lavatory now does not harbour this pest, and there seems to be no way of controlling its spread.

Its unsavoury habits are well observed. Most noteworthy is the loud protesting noise it makes when pressed, a noisy rush of air which effectively drowns all conversation within 20 yards of it. Defenders of the creature maintain that it can be trained to dry one's hands, as the name suggests, but research does not always bear that out. For a start, the rush of air seems in a curious way to turn wet hands even wetter initially. Then, when dryness begins to creep in, the thing suddenly stops emitting air and goes sullen until struck fiercely.

The chief objection, though, is that it does not dry the hands so much as displace the wetness, and its main object is to blow the moisture from the hands up the wrist and soak the sleeve, so that perhaps warm air cuff wetter might be a more accurate name.

Nor does it cater efficiently for the fact that one's face is also wet from washing. In the common or garden warm air hand drier, the rush of air is always directed downwards so that one has to kneel directly underneath it to get the face in the right place, which means that it could also accurately be termed the warm air knee soaker. Later varieties of the beast have an improved nozzle which can be turned upwards, thus purportedly drying the face in a standing position. In fact, the main effect is to drive water up the nostrils and into the eyebrows, from where it is difficult to extract it except with the help of the paper towels which luckily often breed in its vicinity.

A further effect of its face-drying activity is to plunge the hair into disarray, and note well what happens then. One returns to the basin and mirror to comb the hair again.

One then washes one's comb, one hopes. One then finds that the hands are wet again which necessitates another visit to the warm air hand drier at which point one tends to get one's pocket handkerchief out, dry one's hands and make a run for it.

Defenders of the vermin sometimes claim that it operates more hygienically than the domestic roller towel. But is that so? It is well known that however well you wash your hands, you always leave some dirt on the towel. When you dry your hands on the warm air hand drier, *where does that dirt go?*

JOURNALISM PRIZES are all geared to feature-writing, which is, after all, not the same thing as real reporting. In an effort to encourage young reporters everywhere, this column is instituting an annual prize to be given to the best piece of investigative journalism which obeys the following rules:

1. The piece shall be entitled: 'Warehouse Blaze: No Deaths'.

2. The subject of the piece must be a warehouse fire on the edge of a large town in which nobody shall die, but not less than £50,000 worth of damage be caused.

3. Any firemen mentioned in the piece must toil rather than work, and they should be weary rather than tired. They can, if you like, risk their lives again and again. If an inferno is mentioned, it must be a raging one.

4. The piece shall be about 400 words long, of which about 150 will be cut by the judges.

5. The following phrases must appear in the piece:
'Flames shot more than 100ft in the air'; 'Fire brigades from up to 20 miles away were called'; 'Eye witnesses reported a series of explosions'; 'The blaze was eventually brought under control'.

6. State whether arson is suspected or not. If not, do not forget to mention the cigarette stub which almost certainly started the blaze.

7. Report a comment from *either* a weary fire officer who had nothing but praise for the magnificent way his men reacted, *or* a nightwatchman

who was lucky to escape with his life, as the building went up like a powder keg.

8. Extra marks will be given for any local resident who has been warning for years that this sort of thing could happen.

9. Specify to the nearest 10,000 gallons how much water was poured on to the conflagration.

10. Include at least three misprints and one missing line in

11. Entries should either be telephoned direct to the judges, *or* written on small pieces of paper the size of large confetti.

12. The entrants should not use his own name on the piece. It must be signed 'from our own reporters'.

13. The first prize is £100, of which £50 will be paid immediately in taxes and the rest at some future unspecified date.

14. The closing date of the contest is about an hour from now.

THERE WAS a sensation at the Central Criminal Court yesterday when a man who had given his name as Charlie Fingers, who is on trial on charges of impersonation, fraud, conspiracy, corruption and masquerading as a solicitor, went into the dock for the first time. When asked what his profession was, he answered: 'Juryman'.

The prosecuting counsel demanded to know how he could possibly make a living as a juryman. Fingers explained that as an experienced member of a jury he could clear up to £40,000 on one trial by accepting outside commissions.

Counsel: Do you mean—*to affect the outcome of the jury's decision*?

Fingers: Of course.

Counsel: Could you give the jury some idea of how this is done?

Fingers: I'm sure they know already.

Counsel: Nevertheless.

Fingers: Certainly. Recently for example, I sat on the jury during Sir Anthony Lichtenstein's trial for tax evasion, and he slipped me £25,000 to get a verdict of not guilty.

Counsel: Ah! But Sir Anthony was found guilty, was he not?

Fingers: Certainly. That's because I got a better offer of £35,000 from the Stockwell Mob to make sure he went down.

Counsel: The average member of the public is called to serve on a jury no more than once or twice in a lifetime. You cannot be employed very frequently at your disgraceful trade.

20

Fingers: Yes, well, I'm not an average member of the public, am I? They don't like serving on juries, do they? So when a friendly bloke like me comes along and offers to relieve them for a small fee . . . do you see what I'm driving at?

Counsel: I most certainly do.

Fingers: Matter of fact, I had half a mind to serve on the jury in this trial, but then I thought it would look silly, constantly running from the jury box to dock and back again. I'm not as young as I used to be either.

Counsel: Thank you, Mr Fingers. Now that we have heard this dreadful confession from your own lips, I have no doubt this court will inflict the heaviest sentence possible.

Fingers: I wouldn't be too sure about that. What do you say, lads?

Jury Foreman: We're with you to a man, Mr Fingers! And we're all very grateful for you-know-what.

Counsel: My Lord! Did you hear *that*?

Judge: I did. I also happen to know from personal experience that Mr Fingers is man of great largesse, ever willing to help out his fellow humans. We are not here to impugn his honour—we are here to acquit him. Now get on with it!

The trial continues.

NORTH
♠A K Q J 10 9 8 7 6 5 4 3 2
WEST
♥A K Q J 10 9 8 7 6 5 4 3 2
EAST
♦A K Q J 10 9 8 7 6 5 4 3 2
SOUTH
♣A K Q J 10 9 8 7 6 5 4 3 2

THIS UNUSUAL hand was recently dealt at a domestic bridge tounament (Mr and Mrs Elkins versus friends) in Slough.

South, who opened the bidding, was tempted to go straight to seven clubs and shout 'Geronimo!' She would certainly have been justified, but after a short strangled silence she decided not to, for two reasons. 1) It would be more fun to work up gradually. 2) She was already prone to overbidding, and this time her partner would think she really had gone round the twist. So she went for the more modest one club.

21

West for similar reasons went one heart and pinched himself hard. North made a more ambitious asking bid of three spades, which under the Lutomer Convention means: Leave this one to me, kid, and also: Is there any more of that excellent white wine?

When East bid four diamonds, brows were furrowed. West had no diamonds to back East, North could feel his old war wound throbbing dangerously and South did indeed have another bottle of white wine but was loth to admit it. Eventually she went four spades, meaning that there was any amount of cider in the fridge if North could be bothered. West went five hearts and North went to the fridge, where he found the white wine. When he came back he passed, using the Russian Convention to signify that his overall strength was so great he could take out the enemy any time.

East now had a problem. If he made a grand slam in diamonds his partner might over-bid on hearts, in which case he would have a coronary. So he went five trumps, meaning he was awfully strong in all suits. This was a downright lie, but it seemed a nice idea at the time.

South now went for broke and bid seven clubs, a signal that she really did have a good hand this time, not to mention the corkscrew, and would North *please* not waggle his eyebrows as he normally did when South overbid. West promptly went seven hearts and North, after waggling his eye-brows in an extremely annoying fashion, went seven spades.

This left East with a problem. He had the best hand he was ever likely to have in his life and yet he could not bid his own suit. If he went seven no trumps, someone else would lead and he would not get a single trick. If he passed, he could only bring North down, and not get a grand slam. In this situation he did the only possible thing: he threw his cards passionately on the floor and started hitting North over the head with a rolled up newspaper.

Play. Everyone showed their one-suit hand. A furious post-mortem ensued, which ended with East and West storming out of the house. North opened the bottle of white wine and got very drunk, while South went to bed in tears.

Moral. Play pontoon with matches for stakes.

URBAN NATURALIST

THE PHOTO-copy machine is now one of the common-est sights in our cities (writes urban naturalist 'Bin-Liner'). It makes its home most often in offices, but can also now be seen in sub-post offices, stationers, chemists and public libraries. It likes, too, to occupy premises recently vacated by bankrupt tile shops or boutiques.

Naturalists have not yet decided whether the photo-copier is a pest or a useful part of the environment. Its habits are, on the whole, neutral. It feeds on large amounts of money, in return for which it will turn any object offered to it into a vague facsimile of the same object, in any quantity desired. On the evolutionary scale of urban life this is a very primitive function, no more advanced than that of the lesser Box Brownie or common carbon paper, and yet it is much more popular with the public than either of those.

Quite why is difficult to understand in view of its un-doubted anti-social tendencies. These can be classed under three headings.

1: Its ability to attract undesirable company, such as architects wishing to copy complicated plans of drainage, musicians with parts of very advanced chamber pieces, gentlemen with family trees of inconvenient size, and committee members of parent/teacher associations trying to send out 300 invitations to annual general meetings when they know very well that not more than 35 people will attend.

2: Its mischievous habit of disobeying instructions by chewing up the paper it is given. Or sending forth blank pieces of paper instead of copies. Or chopping off the sides of the object it is meant to reproduce. Or delivering copies of objects left by the previous customer. Or making 100 copies when, quite clearly, only one was intended.

3: Its urge to send rude messages in return for kind-ness, such as INSERT MORE PAPER or CALL KEY OPERATOR.

When situated in offices, it seems gifted with telepathic powers with which to boost its anti-social behaviour. That is, it seems to know in advance when you are in a great hurry or have an important document for it to swallow. On those occasions it emits a strong scent of some kind to attract one of the following before your arrival: —

a: A man in overalls with screwdrivers in his pockets, attacking the beast from the side and holding an inky roller in his hands.

b: A person who has never met a photocopier before and does not know how to make friends with the animal.

c: A total stranger feeding the creature with what looks like a very long unpublished novel and who, when questioned, says: 'Our photocopier upstairs has broken down.'

The main clue to its otherwise incomprehensible popularity lies in its having one function only. In an age when urban machines are capable of doing everything from laying out a newspaper to booking your hotel room in Zurich, it's a great relief to have a little creature like the photocopier which does *nothing* except mimic your piece of paper, without telling you the recipe for the day, giving you the rundown on your warehouse or confirming your flight on an overbooked plane. The photocopier may be stupid, limited and mischievious, but at least it will never reveal your previous criminal record to a bent lawyer.

A PRESS conference was called today by the shadow Archbishop of Canterbury, the Left Rev Michael Ramsey McDonald, to explain what he had said about marriage to Tony and Vanessa, two young socialists who had asked him to be in an officiation situation at their wedding. He warned them first that matrimony was an institution ordained by lawyers and begged them to consider changing their minds.

'Finding they had set their hearts on it, I then called the meeting to order. First item on the agenda was whether Vanessa should agree to obey Tony. Well, I put it to them in the strongest possible way that that sort of obedience was a totally outmoded concept based on an elitist, male-oriented view of marriage, and had no place in a modern ongoing partnership. We took a vote and the motion was carried, *nem con.*

'I also proposed that instead of promising to obey Tony, Vanessa should consider promising to "strive to honour executive decisions as reached freely and frankly between them". She promised to consider promising that, and the matter was put forward to a subsequent meeting.'

The Left Rev Michael McDonald explained that he had then disposed in turn of the terms cherish, honour, hold and love, all of which were, in his view, relics of a bourgeois morality.

'I pointed out to them that in all successful marriages there was an agreed arbitration machinery which could be used as a last resort, but that generally speaking most problems were covered by pre-existing agreed consultation methods. When an argument situation crops up in marriage, it is not much good shouting: "You promised to cherish me!". You have got to get round the table and thrash it out, person to person.

'And there would be arguments. Make no mistake about that. Marriage, I told them, is a bit like our great Labour Party, you know. We wrangle and we fight, but this only stresses the great underlying unity of the movement. The coming together of man and woman is like the joining together of left-winger and moderate—different views serving one end. The only sin was to lust after other parties, and I reminded them that even if they had only done so in their hearts, they had committed the sin as much as if they had stood against Labour at Warrington.'

And had he talked to them about, um, sex?

'Well, time was getting on by then, so we deferred that to the next meeting. I closed with a few words asking them to sell all that they had and give unto the socially disadvantaged, and they promised to refer back to their executive. But I think you can say that progress was definitely made and I am not unhopeful of the outcome.'

COME WITH me, come with me through the foaming molecules of time, past unimaginable distances, to the farthest end of the Kosmorss and the heavenly body of Karlsagan. Through swirling adjectives and belts of poison gas we dimly see the enormous dome as it rises into vision, that enormous domelike head covered with fine black hair millions of years ago and combed sideways a minute before filming. Nothing moves on that great dome, not the huge, petrified eyebrows which have been there for the aeons of time since the programme started, not those twin pools of optic nerves which stare unblinking across space and into our homes, only that open hole we call the mouth, which moves constantly day and night and out of which come the most clotted prose known to the galaxy.

OK, Jack, it's been 50 seconds since we saw a rocket blast off. Let 'em have it. Thanks.

What goes on inside the gigantic dome we call Karlsagan? What labyrinths of steamy thought, what hissing fissures of molten gerunds and superheated participles combine to whistle at the speed of sleep through the open hole we call the mouth, in one ear and out the other? Well, frankly, we don't know. We just buy the programme from America, where apparently it has done awfully well. We should have seen it first, I suppose. Too late now.

Meanwhile, another vast wave of particles starts its endless voyage across the Kosmorss, from the vast dome we call Karlsagan, where the letter R is scarcely known, and when those particles have finished their terrifyingly lonely voyage through the infinite vacuum called international syndication, they are decoded in tiny receivers through the earth we call Earth, and nobody is any the wiser. This is the gift, the gift of Karlsagan, the tree of the absolute lack of knowledge, in another time scale altogether where a 40-minute programme can last for billions of years.

OK, Jack, the spaceship simulator. Some molten lava. And a shot of the Arizona desert labelled 'Just like Mars'. That should keep 'em happy.

Is there any life on Karlsagan? That endless process that we call 'language', does it betoken any form of thought or intelligence? When it says 'careening through the valleys of Mars', and we know, because we've looked it up in the dictionary, that 'careen' means to turn a ship on its side and give it a good scrub, does this mean that language on Karlsagan is dead and lifeless?

There is much we do not know. There are questions still to be asked. Is there anything good on the other side? Will you wake me at the end of this? How much did the BBC pay for this? Science is still very young and cannot begin to grapple with these questions. But this we do know. With this knob here we can simply push and the pictures will disappear. The vast dome will shrink to a tiny dot and go away. The mystery of the eyebrows cannot come back till next week.

OK, Jack. They've all switched off. You can bring up the credits now. Let's detonate them with a final shot of galactic energy. Wow! Pam! Kerrunch! Yawn. Zzzzzz.

FROM A train window I spotted the other day, between Stafford and Nuneaton, a vast development site on which only one thing had so far been erected, a very large sign reading 'CENTRAL PARCEL RESORTATION COMPLEX'. I fell to musing, as one tends to when a new word like resortation swims along, and while I was musing the following scene wrote itself before my very eyes.

(The offices and workshops of Billboard and Flyblown, old-fashioned sign painters. Billboard is an elderly craftsman, suffering from VAT elbow. So is Flyblown. They do one-off signs. Remember 'Great Cressingford By-Pass: Opening Spring, 1981'. That was one of theirs. They were also called in to modernize it so that it read, 'Opening Autumn 1982'. Billboard is studying an office memo.)

Billboard: Brenda took down an order for a sign last night over the phone. Central Parcel Resortation Complex. From the Post Office, I imagine.

Flyblown: There's no such word as Resortation.

Billboard: That's what Brenda took down.

Flyblown: You know Brenda.

Billboard: You know the Post Office.

Flyblown: You know what I think? I think it's meant to be Central Parcel *Restoration* Complex. It's going to be a new intensive care unit for damaged packages, where loving craftsmen will repair the injury done to them by high-spirited postmen at Crewe Station, and where Victorian parcels which the Post Office has not got round to delivering this century will be beautifully restored with authentic string.

Billboard: Sometimes I think you're totally out of touch with reality, Flyblown.

Flyblown: All right—suggest a better theory.

Billboard: I think the word Brenda heard as 'resortation' is actually 'recitation'.

Flyblown: When did you last hear a parcel recite?

Billboard: Not parcel—*Purcell*. Central Purcell Recitation Complex. I imagine the Purcell Room is expanding its operations. Another Purcell Room opening in your area soon! Try a Purcell-burger tonight! Take away a Big P.

Flyblown: The Purcell Room is not a recitation room—it's a recital room. Recitation is poetry, or prose, as it's now called.

Billboard: Then it must be the Central Pearsall Recitation Complex.

Flyblown: I've got it! You remember all those free rail offers on the washing powder packets?

Billboard: Ye-e-es.

Flyblown: It's the Central Persil Re-Station Complex!

Billboard: Unless it's a hospital.

Flyblown: Hospital?

Billboard: Essential Person Resuscitation Complex.

Flyblown: Look, I haven't got time to sit around all day. Can you do the sign?

Billboard: Sadly not. You remember the sign I did for that penthouse flat in Mayfair three years ago? 'Luxury Flat—Would Suit Arab Millionaire Only'?

Flyblown: Well?

Billboard: It's still unsold and now it's been condemned because of dry rot *and* damp.

Flyblown: The flat?

Billboard: The sign. I'm doing it again today.

Flyblown: Then I'll do Central Parcel Resortation Complex.

Billboard: You'll use those words?

Flyblown: Of course. What does it matter? Nobody ever reads them anyway.

MOST OF us like visiting old castles now and again. Most of us hate buying the historical leaflet that goes with them, usually because we bought it once years ago and have still got it at home somewhere. Today's all-purpose guide is designed to fit almost every castle and to replace all known leaflets.

THIS EDIFICE, though not quite as imposing as Pembroke, Dover or Warwick, or indeed quite as interesting, historical or well preserved, does have its own points of interest and is, in its own particular way, equally imposing and historical, though not quite so well preserved.

There was a small wooden structure here in Saxon days, of which nothing now remains. The natural defensive properties of the site recommended themselves to William I, who gave it to his kinsman Hugh de Beurre. De Beurre, created First Earl of Sandwich, erected a motte and a bailey with incredible rapidity, threw up a keep, flung round it a curtain wall and peppered the moat with swans. Emboldened by his success, he rose against the King, was defeated and saw the castle razed to the ground. Nothing now remains of it.

The site next passed into the ownership of Raoul de Brioche, an accountant who had been of much help to the King in preparing his tax returns. Careful not to make the same mistakes as de Beurre, Brioche very slowly constructed a square castle with a round tower at each corner, spread over several years in order to minimize tax liability. The building was completed in the eleventh century with the addition of the enormous gatehouse, of which little now remains except the modern postcard kiosk.

The walls of the towers were so massively thick (except for arrow slits so placed that defenders could fire playfully at the next tower) that there was no room inside for living space, and all the castle occupants were forced to live in the great hall together. Little now remains of the walls except a vague musty smell.

The Brioche family ran into financial difficulties in the fourteenth century (the King noticed they had more money than he did and took it) and the castle passed into the possession of Crouton, Rothschild, Baguette and Profiterole, a medieval firm of estate agents specializing in short wartime lets.

They added a small luxury set of apartments on the north side, with en suite privies as well as a private chapel, of which all that remains now is a sign reading SITE OF CHAPEL. After the disastrous holiday season of 1486, the castle was sold to the Pain family who turned it into a second country castle for weekends.

It was still in their possession at the outbreak of the Civil War, when Sir Bruno Pain set off to serve the King. In 1648 the castle was attacked by Parliamentary forces, but after an heroic 60-day siege in which the garrison was ably led by Lady Pain they were beaten off. The castle was then besieged by Royalists, whom she also repulsed. By now an experienced campaigner, she subsequently beat off attacks by Puritans, Seventh Day Adventists, National Art Collections Fund and finally by Sir Bruno himself, come to reclaim his own. In the ensuing reconciliation the castle was almost totally destroyed, thus leaving the modern shell we know so well.

For the next two centuries the remains of the castle were used exclusively for the cultivation of ivy and nettles, before being taken over as a depot by a local coal and coke company; to this day, the fortunate sightseer may find the occasional valuable lump of Victorian solid fuel.

Now carefully preserved, little remains of the original structure except the imposing south-east tower, once much taller, and an interesting chamber by the modern gentlemen's lavatory, whose function is unknown, but visitors will not fail to sense the grandeur of the medieval castle and the rich historical aroma of the whole site.

Though not quite as fine as some more famous, this is indeed, a castle to savour and, above all, to enjoy. Price 50p. Admission £1.50. Open 2–4 pm on Fridays throughout the summer.

☎ THE MOREOVER ADVICE SERVICE

YOU MAY have noticed that the once wide open spaces of British corridors are now filled at ten-yard intervals by fire doors. As there is some incomprehension among the public about the reasons, I have been asked to bring this little pamphlet to your attention.

Q What is a fire door?
A It is a door placed in a corridor to fuel the flames of a big fire.

Q Hold on. Aren't fire doors made of hard-to-burn material?
A Yes. So are metal ships, concrete buildings and brick houses. They, too, are burning down the whole time.

Q Hmm. What other functions do fire doors perform?
A They stop people running away from fires in a disorderly fashion, constantly forcing them to slow down and open doors.

Q What does it mean when it says PUSH on a fire door?
A It means that it says PUSH on the other side as well.

Q Why is there a small window in fire doors?
A So that you can see the person coming the other way who is going to reach the door at exactly the same moment as you.

Q Who has the right of way in that case?
A The person pushing the tea trolley, carrying the tray or steering the cabinet of documents.

Q Who is that?
A Always the other person.

Q Why, next to the sign saying PUSH, is there a handle for pulling?'
A So that you can pull open the door for the trolleyperson.

Q What happens then?
A You realize that your arms are not long enough to open the other door as well, so the trolleyperson tries to deal with that and you all become hopelessly stuck.

Q And burnt to death?
A No, no. People working near by are aware of the threat posed by fire doors and are careful not to cause fires.

Q But if they did?
A The fire brigade would be summoned.

Q Would they put the fire out?
A No. Their access would be blocked by fire doors.

Q Where are fire doors generally placed?
A In hotels, large offices, leisure centres and at the top of short flights of steps.

Q Where do fires generally occur?
A The same places.

Q Do fire doors have any earthly use at all?
A Yes. They have helped to stamp out sexual discrimination.

Q Could you explain that?

30

A Certainly. Before the advent of fire doors, it was customary for men to open doors for women.

Q *Really?*

A You are probably too young. Anyway, they found that if men stopped the whole time to open fire doors for women, they never got anywhere, so the custom lapsed and men and women are now on a totally equal footing in a door-opening situation.

Q *Would not it be more common sense, then, to call them sex equality doors?*

A Common sense has nothing to do with it.

Q *What is the solution to the fire door problem?*

A To wedge them permanently open.

'IT'S LIKE a fairy tale,' said the American lady. 'Only the British can do it this way,' said the *Tokyo Evening News*. 'Es mucho hombre,' they were saying throughout Latin America. Yes, over 750 million people are thought to have been glued to their sets as Ian Botham single-handed rescued England yet again from disaster. What a man! What a giant! Wearing that flowing white shirt (exclusively designed for him by the exclusive chemisiers, Gavin and Lavinia Sportskit) and his flowing brown George V beard, this titan of modern television pounded in again and again, hurled the ball down the pitch and turned away in agony as it missed bat, wicket and pad.

This is the kind of simple but moving ritual that the British still do best. Who can ever forget those images? Botham, leaping high in the air in triumph. Botham, standing silently and reverently in the slips beside Mike Brearley, his father. Botham, a stump held aloft in the final act as he says the all-important words with an endearing fluff: 'That's how!' Then the slow-motion replays. (Please reread this paragraph.)

It seemed as if the whole population of Birmingham was there to greet their idol. Some had slept out the night before rolled in Union Jacks, some had queued all morning at the local off-licence, but all came together in one vast crowd as they simply but movingly flowed across the field and trampled the pitch underfoot, which for four days had not given a great deal of help to the bowlers or batsmen, though the occasional one lifted sharply, didn't it, Trevor?

Yes, Brian, and I think it's worth pointing out that with men like Botham around, it shows that Britain cannot yet be counted out. Of course, there's still a great deal to do and it's up to Ian now to consolidate Britain's position, safeguard our herring stocks in the North Sea, turn back the flood of Golden Delicious apples and get the economy on a sound footing. But given what he has done already, there's no reason why he should not do this as well. Now let's have another look at That Shirt.

Meanwhile in America, where they have taken this handsome prince of cricket to their hearts, there are secret plans to transfer Botham to Broadway. 'We have nothing in the States like your ancient cricket ceremony,' says Hal Prince, who is widely tipped to become Henry V, 'not even baseball at the moment. And those flowing helmets with their simple plastic visors—it's just so medieval. And to think that an event like that can take place today without anyone shooting at least an umpire.'

Yet as the euphoria recedes and the Union Jacks are packed up to go to Old Trafford and the Edgbaston groundsman tears his hair out at the sight of the pitch, let us not forget that cricket is, after all, only a game and that the true business of Britain still remains: to get Ovett and Coe back breaking records. But just for a moment let us savour the great moment again and have a last look at That Shirt and That Stump.

STOP PRESS: Mr Ian Botham has been formally charged by the Birmingham police with taking a stump, the property of the MCC. 'In these lawless days,' says the Chief Constable, 'it is our duty to stamp out looting and rioting wherever it occurs.' World reaction to the arrest was immediate. 'Your British law is still the best in the world,' said an American woman simply but movingly. 'I shall be over for the trial, that's for sure.'

From time to time, the Radio Times goes on strike. This summary of one day's radio programmes can be cut out and kept for any future day.

Radio One
As Radio Two

Radio Two
As Radio One

Radio Three
6.55 am Weather
Debussy Overnight Rain
7.0 News
Benn Four Prognostications,
Patricia Hughes (contralto)
7.5 Morning Concert
Pumpernickel The Yeast Ascending
POLISH SOLIDARITY ORCHESTRA
conducted by the Pope
7.16* **Brearley** Four English Folk Songs: The Heavy Roller, Away in the Outfield, 'Twas a Merry Umpire, The Moving of the Screen
7.27 Alpen Morning Overture
THE LUCERNE STRINGS
conducted by
Jean-Pierre Roughage
8.0 News
Benn Four Prognostications
(repeat)
8.5 Emmanuel Wedding Suite
THE ROYAL ENSEMBLE
8.14* **Boizot** Three Pizzas in the Italian Style
8.39* **Haydn** Symphony no 108
(The 'Repeat')
BBC YESTERYEAR ORCHESTRA
conducted by the late
Edmund Rubato
9.0 News
9.5 This Week's Composer
Hertz van Rental

Some of the Dutch composer's most famous songs, including Weekend Cortina and Unlimited Mileage.
10.0 The Song Recital
11.0 The Organ Recital
11.45 Midday Concert
Given in our Tewkesbury studio in front of an invited listener by the BBC Welterweight Orchestra
1.0 News
1.5 A Gramophone Record
2.0 Another Gramophone Record
2.30 The Same Gramophone Record (this time played at the right speed)
3.30 Albanian Piano Music
3.35 A Concert of Organic Music
The Schola Musica Alfalfa play natural music by Soya, Mung, Flageolet, Pulse and Fenugreek on 100% wholewood instruments
5.0 Caught in a Traffic Jam
Music to listen to in first gear
7.0 Waiting for the Prom
(on gramophone records: repeat)
7.30 Tonight's Prom
Mozart A Very Easy Piece
Karl-Heinz Beanz A Very Hard Piece
8.30* Interval Drink
8.50* Prom: Part Two
Beethoven A Very Long Piece
10.00 The Other Arts
A programme for people who cannot stand music
11.15 Close-down

Radio Four
Repeat (see last week for details)

TODAY IS the Glorious Twelfth, acclaimed by game birds everywhere as the day they finally go out and do battle with the British Association of Shooting and Conservation.

Everywhere partridges and grouse, pheasants and ptarmigan have been eagerly clawing the ground while the antiquated British laws have prevented them until now from pitting their wits against the impoverished aristocrats and migrating Japanese businessmen who are their natural enemy.

Armed only with tiny firearms against the massed battalions of the air, the pitifully small number of shooters in the Scottish hills have all our sympathy and support on this occasion.

However, there is a less serious side to the occasion and that is the race to bring back the first casualties on the birds' side to London for ceremonial eating with full honours. For in this war, as in Africa so many years ago, it is customary to eat your enemy.

The birds are normally sent down by rail from Scotland and thus arrive on English tables within three or four days, but this year some ingenious ideas are being tried out for the first time. The Majestic Hotel restaurant is hiring a team of crack shots to travel on the early train from Scotland before they have even shot a bird, with rifles sticking out of the window. As soon as they have sighted and brought down a couple of braces they will pull the communication cord, jump off, jump back on and continue.

And if they don't shoot any birds? 'We shall pull the communication cord several times,' their team manager says. 'It won't help us at all, but it's going to hinder a lot of other people and that's the main thing.'

The Smart Place of Walton Street have gone one better in the Partridge Nouveau Race, as it is called. They have spent the last six months training a pair of grouse to fly from Scotland to Belgravia where they will be shot and served on arrival. Isn't this a little ungrateful though?

'Well, they are ungrateful little beggars themselves,' top chef Pierre says. 'We've done 10 test flights already and they've only arrived promptly on five occasions. On two occasions they took the slow train from Dundee and three times they went straight to the North British Hotel in Edinburgh and stayed there. Which is a bit disturbing. I personally shall be glad to be shot of the pests.'

Other plans include attempts to gun down birds from helicopters, though this is disapproved of by purists, and to build a small replica of a Scottish moorland near a restaurant outside Guildford in the hope of tempting some expatriate game birds.

But undoubtedly the most daring plan is that of the SAS mess to airlift a chef and mobile kitchen up to Scotland and to drop them on the moors, together with four volunteer diners.

This unusual phenomenon should be seen in the Northern skies shortly after dawn and will take the form of black dots falling from the clouds, followed by flashes of hand grenades, a most appetizing smell, and finally a bill for two of about £1,300 each.

Expensive, but well worth the trip.

TO CELEBRATE the start of a new soccer season, we are proud to publish extracts from one of the earliest football documents known. Written in the early 1880s, it is the journal of a Doncaster Albion fan named Verity Todd. All we know about it is that it was found in an attic last year, is to be published soon by Dutch Elm Books as *The Diary of a Victorian Football Fan* and will make them a quick fortune. These extracts are exclusive to *The Times*, and will be published whenever they can be fitted into an already over-crowded journalistic fixture list. The first one covers the start of the 1881 season of the now defunct Doncaster Albion.

Aug 31, 1881. Rain. Only seven days to kick-off. Jabez Thwaite has been sacked as manager of Albion, and has gone back down the mines. Serve him right, I say. Anyone who can lose a close season friendly against Market Rasen Stableboys 7—1 must have a question mark against him, that he must.

Sept 1. Mud. New manager is a man named Garnforth, a foreigner from Rotherham way. His pay is said to be £4 ten shilling a year. No manager is worth that sort of fortune.

Sept 2. Fog. After being found drunk at the market, Mr Garnforth the new manager has been relieved of his duties and sent for six months to York Prison. He is said to have received a golden handshake of 15 pence.

Sept 3. It has been announced at the Town Hall this morning that Sir Joshua Bainbridge the Mayor has acted according to his rights and appointed himself manager of Doncaster Albion, to prevent further civil unrest. He will not manage the team himself, being over 80 and bedridden, but has nominated his coachman James to overlook training.

Sept 4. Floods. Several men were swept away in training this morning and James, Sir Joshua's coachman, was drowned. I fear this does not augur well for Albion's new season. It is said that Mr Garnforth has escaped from the prison at York and there is a great hue and cry. I pray that he is not reappointed manager.

Sept 5. Mr Jabez Thwaite has been brought back from the mines to be the new manager. A small crowd gathered outside the ground this morning, crying for him to be deported, but they were quick dispersed by musket shot. Jos Bawtry, our left wing forward, has gone down with the cholera, but should be fit for Saturday.

Sept 6. Mr Thwaite has publicly promised a mixture of quality play and entertainment in the new season. This has disappointed the public, who were hoping for bloodshed. Tomorrow is the first match, against the Barnsley Philosophical Society, who are well known as hard men. My mother has promised to have my new knitted scarf ready.

Sept 7. Funeral in the morning of James, late coachman and manager. Not many casualties. In the afternoon the first fixture of the season, which draws a record crowd of 365. At halftime we draw one each, Harry Michaelmas's opportunist goal being answered by a penalty shot from Barnsley after Sidebotham ill-advisedly broke a bottle over the head of one of their men. In the dying minutes of the game Barnsley score a second goal when our goalkeeper's cap falls over his eyes and becomes entangled with his moustache. We stream from the ground in disgust. Matters are not made better when the Doncaster Pink One prints the following dubious headline: 'Barnsley Philosophical Society Ask All the Questions', though we are heartened later to hear that Mr Jabez Thwaite has again been deposed as manager and forcibly enlisted in the Yorkshire Fusiliers for three years.

YESTERDAY I received a letter addressed to Miles Kingston, a sure sign that it was from someone who has not known me more than two years. Imagine my surprise when I found that it was from Lord Illegible, a total stranger, and that it contained an offer of such generosity that it would be criminal not to pass it on to readers.

Here it is, in toto.

Dear Sir,

You may have read in the past few years about a series of art robberies of the most daring nature. You may have noticed that in each case a work was stolen which could never be resold on the open market, so well known is it. And you may have wondered at the time, who is the lucky art collector who is going to enjoy these masterpieces in the privacy of his own home?

The answer is—you!

Yes, we invite you to become a member of the World Masterpiece Club which, for an entrance fee of a mere £400,000, will allow you to enjoy the greatest works of art in the privacy of your own home.

A panel of the most exquisitely tasteful art connoisseurs have chosen the paintings that they personally think would add lustre to your drawing room without being too overpowering, or clashing with the Ming.

A team of the most skilled art thieves in the world, all of whom have studied for three years in Italy, have been working full-time to secure these masterpieces, taking care not to deplete any collection noticeably. (Some curators have expressed their private gratitude to us for thinning out over-rich displays.)

A squad of the finest carpenters available have been working non-stop for two years to create the finest hand-carved crates in which to pack these chefs-d'oeuvre, with special attention to humidity control and security precautions.

So attentive are we to standards that in some cases where we are not satisfied with the quality of the works in question, we have taken steps to return them. You may have read about our recent dissatisfaction with the Dulwich Rembrandt.

Now at last we are ready to pass on to you, our hand-selected art-lover, the fruits of our labour. All you have to do is write back specifying an appointment and a hand-picked team of surveyors and interior decorators will call to inspect your walls and advise on the choice of painting. They will be accompanied by an accredited Swiss financier who will personally inspect your cheque and take it away for certain tests. If you prefer to pay in cash, we will send a small unmarked van to anywhere in the Cayman Islands, Liechtenstein or Jersey.

This is, of course, an exclusive offer and we would prefer you not to pass on details to friends of yours. We shall be getting in touch with them separately.

> Yours very sincerely,
> Lord Illegible

PS: To whet your appetite, I enclose, absolutely free, a small watercolour by James Whistler. Delicieux, n'est-ce-pas? If you decide not to avail yourself of our offer, do not bother to return the Whistler; we shall come round one night when you are asleep and collect it.

If any reader who is tempted by this opportunity cares to get in touch with me, I shall send off his application with mine. To make things easier, make your cheques for £400,000 payable to me.

STARTLING NEW evidence has come to light to suggest that world records in athletics are getting worse, not better, and that Sebastian Coe may be one of the slowest milers of all time.

Dr Pocket-Sinclair, newly appointed statistician with the England football team and probably the only man who can now get them into the World Cup finals, thoroughly agrees with this theory which he invented.

'Only in the most abstruse and unreal sense is it true to say that Seb Coe can run a mile in less than 3.48,' he told me over a slice of lemon at the Half-Time Rocket, the England team's local pub. 'It is more true to say that he has done it once, on a special surface, with special pacers, in special weather conditions, *after a year's special training*. So it is even more true to say that it took Coe over a year to run a mile in 3.48. Now in the old days, when training was more realistic, it took a man only a month or two to break a world record. That, by any standards, is a much faster time.'

Another man who goes along with this theory is Dr Adidas, behavioural scientist at the Institute of Advanced Sports Injuries. Dr Adidas, who recently changed his name at the suggestion of his sponsors, feels that modern athletics is quickly losing touch with the real world in common with other things like stamp collecting and sociology.

'Athletics used to be a sport in which people attempted to do everyday things like running and jumping, but faster and higher than usual. Now it is an almost totally impractical amusement like *It's A Knock-Out*. You see, if the organizers of *It's A Knock-Out* devised an event in which competitors had to launch themselves backwards, lying on their backs, over a thin bar and then land on a huge foam rubber cushion, the contestants would think they had gone too far. But call it the high jump and the Fosbury Flop, and nobody even questions it.

'I also dispute the theory that today's athletes are the fittest people in the world. In fact, they are more subject to physical disability than anyone else. The slightest twinge or strain is enough to eliminate them from their chosen activity, the sort of ailment that you or I would take in our stride. Athletes are not only getting slower, they are also getting unfitter.'

Yet another expert who goes along with the theory, or at least would like to get in on the act, is the popular Cockney palaeontologist, 'Cocker' Leakey.

'See, yer actual modern athlete is a freak, a Darwinian irrelevance. I have recently discovered a knee-cap over six million years old, from which I have deduced that early man could run like the clappers without any training at all; and not just selected members of the tribe, but the whole blooming lot of them. Usually they had a sabre-toothed tiger right behind them. Actually, the tiger could run faster than them, but on the other hand he couldn't eat them all at once, so he'd just gobble up the tail-enders. Survival of the fastest, we call it.

'What's missing from modern athletics is that sort of panic and sheer terror which kept early man on his toes. I wouldn't half mind seeing how well Coe could do with a sabre-toothed tiger right behind him. But I expect it's against the ruddy rules of modern so-called athletics.'

In the light of those expert opinions, Moreover Enterprises Limited have reluctantly decided that they will not be sponsoring Coe or Ovett in the foreseeable future.

THE MOREOVER ADVICE SERVICE

WITH AUTUMN nearly here, summer is nearly over and that means that gardening correspondents all over the country are getting out the article they wrote this time last year and rephasing it slightly. In the absence of a filing system, I am forced to fall back on personal experience. I hope readers will bear with me.

That bright feature of the summer garden, the barbecue, is now in its last few days and it is time to bring it indoors again. Simply detach all the metal parts from each other (you will find the instructions in that pile of newspapers you put on the bonfire last week) and put them, together with any leftover charcoal, under the stairs. This will enable you, the next time the light fails under the stairs, to go in there with a new bulb, fall over the barbecue and come out with your hands black.

Dig over the barbecue patch, rake it and plant with Sperring's Fireproof Grass.

Deck-chairs should be washed, scraped and varnished, but just stack them under the stairs as usual. If you have a tennis court, now is the time to lift old tennis balls from the herbaceous border. If you planted a badminton net on the lawn in early spring, you should now unravel it and place it under the stairs; your local fisherman will be glad to help you with this.

If you have a fish pond, this is the best time of year to dredge it for deck-chairs, old tennis balls, missing barbecue pieces, headless corpses, etc. In my experience, the local sub-aqua club always enjoys the chance to explore a new place. Swimming pools should be emptied, cleaned, checked for punctures, rolled up, and placed beneath the stairs.

The luckier among you may have follies, grottoes or ruins at the bottom of your garden, and it's always worth checking to see if they are well maintained and in good order.

If they are, give them a quarter of an hour's vandalizing till they are looking their old selves. A simple hammer is probably the best tool, but for the gardener in a hurry, Sperring's Folly Gunpowder is very good.

Now is the time to start thinking about getting your lawn-mower overhauled. Now is the time to remember that after you got it overhauled last year, it broke down on the first mowing day of spring. Now is the time to decide to sell your lawn-mower and buy a new one next year.

If you have a garden of the more extensive kind, you probably have a herd of deer, and this is the time of year to count them all again to see if the breeding season has gone well, or alternatively if you bought all females by mistake. Deer counting is a time-consuming process and I often find that the local primary school geography class is glad to take over this duty.

If you have made any major changes to your estate this summer, now is the time to notify the Ordnance Survey.

If it is open to members of the public, now is the time to check the estate for missing members of the public. I find that the members of the local CID are always glad to muck in with this job, as a day out from the office.

If you have any time left over, glance over the borders to see if the flowers need dead-heading. The latest poll conducted by *The Times* Top Ten Think Tank people shows that the following are the 10 most favourite dead flowers in British gardens:

1. Giant Hog Fennel, 2. Monk's Curfew, 3. Alma Mater, 4. Lady's After-Shave, 5. Common Salt 'n' Vinegar. 6. Wild Barbecue Pickle, 7. Gloria Mundi, 8. Indelible Blue Felt Tips, 9. Aspersions, 10. Virginia Filters.

Correction: *In last week's gardening notes I should, of course, have written 'Now is the time to prune shoots' and not 'Now is the time to shoot prunes'.*

WHEN I turn my radio to a new waveband I generally encounter complete silence or interference. I have now discovered that silence means that the BBC has stopped doing one thing and not decided what to do next; and that interference is not interference but applause for what the BBC has just done. The time I spend waiting to find out what's happening is only minutes in Earth time, but is hours of agony by any other reckoning—or was until I devised this analytical chart to help one know in a flash what kind of silence or applause was involved.

1. Dead silence. This means that someone has just said: 'But for more news of that shock defeat, let's go straight over to Brian in New York...' The tape recording which Brian made an hour earlier has then malfunctioned.

2. Dead, reverent silence. This is heard only on Radio 3 and forms part of the respectful minute and a half that announcers always leave after the end of a piece of music before telling you what it was.

3. A splashy, percussive noise, as of ten veal escalopes being beaten in an echoey room. What it actually is is a couple of dozen people trying to clap hard enough to sound like a hundred. It usually occurs at the end of music recitals marked in the Radio Times as 'given before an invited audience'.

4. The distressing sound of a ward in a consumptive hospital. This tells you at once that you have landed in a concert between movements, and reflects the English belief that clapping will disturb musicians but choking to death won't.

5. A never-ending rainstorm. This is the end-of-concert ovation from an audience determined at any cost to drag an encore from an artist who wouldn't dream of leaving without doing three.

6. Loud, hysterical laughter. From a comedy show, of course, but not just any comedy show. The laughter was performed 10 years ago by an unknown American audience laughing at an unknown American comic, and has now been exhumed for a BBC programme called *Golden Comedy Hour*.

7. Loud, firm, even stern appluase. You have just turned to *Any Questions*, where one of the panellists has correctly guessed the communal prejudice of the audience, and has just stated it.

8. A scratchy silence, interspersed occasionally with a faint voice saying 'Hello? hello?' You have tuned into a phone-in programme at the very moment when Kevin of Ealing has been asked to put his question but simply cannot believe that he is on the air.

9. Squeaks, followed by cheers, then more squeaks and more cheers. You are listening to a piano being moved in the Albert Hall.

10. The word 'Well', followed by silence. This is part of *Gardeners' Question Time*. One of the experts is about to disagree totally with the previous expert and is savouring the moment ahead with silent relish.

11. An embarrassed silence. Another Radio 3 speciality. The 33 rpm disc which has been playing for 10 minutes at 45 rpm has just been faded out, and the announcer is composing an apology in his head.

12. A domestic silence, enlivened only by the sound of chairs creaking, spoons being rattled or someone clearing his throat but not speaking. You have arrived in the middle of a Beckett play. If the noises are quite lively, it might even be Pinter.

13. Any other kind of silence. The station you want is off the air. Or, if you are looking for the World Service, they are just switching languages, and you are listening to the three French people tiptoeing out of a studio as three Rumanians tiptoe in.

WHERE WOULD *you* like the third London airport to be? Here is a list of the possible contenders.

☐ **Stansted:** Favoured by the present GLC administration because it would bring lots of jobs (porters, thieves, diamond smugglers, etc) to an area of London where there are a lot of marginal Labour seats, and thus convert airport workers into London voters.

☐ **Maplin:** These lonely sands by the mouth of the River Crouch are a sanctuary for teeming bird life, and many local inhabitants would favour an airport as being less noisy. Burnham is a popular yachting centre, too, and most sailors want the airport to be at Maplin so they can fly up at weekends and avoid the dreadful drive through Essex.

☐ **Brixton:** An airport in Brixton would bring much needed employment to the area and give a chance to redevelop it, quite apart from being bang on the Victoria Line. The noise would be considerable, but, in the words of one supporter of the idea, no worse than a reggae evening.

☐ **Namibia:** A radical site suggested by enlightened areas at County Hall. Although further from London than either Gatwick or Heathrow, it would bring employment, raise British stock in Africa and provide a much-needed international airport for Namibia.

☐ **Wormwood Scrubs:** Very close to the heart of London, this open space at the moment contains only 548 soccer pitches. Experts reckon that football will have been phased out by 1985, especially if we fail to qualify for the World Cup finals, and the ground will be empty by then. The site is adjacent to the Grand Union Canal and the Inland Waterways Board have already drawn up plans for the world's first airport/canal/city centre route via fast water-buses.

☐ **The Thames Estuary:** It would require little extra modification to turn the Thames barrage, now under construction, into a series of runways. Study of other airports surrounded by water (Gibraltar, Hong Kong) show that the percentage of watery landings is very low. And an airport built on water would not be subject to rates, traffic regulations or parking fines, though of course the Port of London Authority would have to charge overnight mooring fees.

☐ **Toxteth:** Much favoured by Mr Michael Heseltine.

☐ **Slough:** Much favoured by Sir John Betjeman.

☐ **The Royal Parks:** Opposed by every conservation group and political party, but favoured by the Royal Family, who would give their eye teeth to pilot planes down into their own back yard.

☐ **Heathrow:** It is technically feasible to build a third airport on top of the first airport, on stilts. It would involve no further clearing of land, no spoiling of amenities, no break-up of communities. It is almost the perfect idea. It is only opposed by those who say that the whole point of building a third airport is not having to go to Heathrow, probably the most powerful lobby in the land.

Just tick your selection in the box provided and send in your entry, saying in not more than 3,000 words why you will continue to travel by train wherever possible.

―――――――――――――――――――――――――――――――――

VENICE, A large town in Northern Italy which is half-covered at high tide. The camera pans across the Pizza San Marco, a wide space dotted here and there with mushrooms, anchovies and extra pepperoni. More ravishing shots of the Palazza Mario e Franco, the Church of the Blessed Placido Domingo, the Tomb of the Unknown Gondolier, etc.

Medium shot of Von Aschenbecker, a German composer on holiday, walking along reading the paper. A cheery Italian passer-by calls out: 'Nice morning, Mr Von Aschenbecker!' He does not even look up.

Passer-by: 'What a curmudgeon, that Van Aschenbecker.'

Second passer-by: 'I can remember him when he was Dirk Bogarde.'

First: 'I can remember Dirk Bogarde when he was Liszt.'

Second: 'I was an ostler in that film.'

First: 'Really? I was only a friend of the groom.'

Von Aschenbecker continues his walk, ignoring greetings and

the furious hootings of gondolas alike. We hear his interior monologue. 'All right, so I'm deaf. Who needs a deaf composer? But then, Beethoven was deaf, and Smetana was deaf too. Both great men. On the other hand, I've been deaf from birth. At least I'll be famous for writing the loudest symphonies in history.'

Mahler's Ninth swells to a climax on the soundtrack. More ravishing shots of the canals of Venice, Lago di Handel etc. They are so beautifully shot that they could be paintings. A small red smudge in the bottom right-hand corner of the screen is, on closer inspection, the signature of one J. M. W. Turner. Good Lord, they *are* paintings!

Von Aschenbecker stops dead in his tracks. He has just seen the most beautiful boy in the world. He muses off-screen: 'What unearthly beauty. I cannot imagine anything more perfect. He could inspire me to write a cantata for huge orchestra, choir and boy soloist into which I could pour my most aesthetic longings. On the other hand, of course, I could just seduce him. Unfortunately, it's not that kind of film.'

Lingering shots of the boy. Lingering shots of more canals. Shots of Von Aschenbecker lingering. More of Mahler's Ninth, to indicate the passing of two weeks. Finally the lonely composer plucks up the courage to address the vision of loveliness.

Von A: 'Excuse me, but I couldn't help noticing how lovely you are. I'm only a poor repressed German composer but I've got some pretty interesting manuscripts back in my room that you might like to see.'

Boy: (speaks rapidly in a foreign language. Subtitles say: 'I'm sorry, but I'm a stranger from Yugoslavia.')

Late-night film advertised at the Gate Cinema, Notting Hill, London. [Moreover Productions proudly present the abridged screenplay of this rare classic.]

Von A: 'Tadzio, eh? That's a cute kind of name. Well, don't forget the invitation.'

Close-up of Von Aschenbecker furiously at work in his room. He is writing a great fugue on the letters of his loved one's name. Unfortunately, there is no note called Z. He determines next time to fall for someone called Abe or Dag. There is a knock at his door.

Hotel manager: 'Sorry to disturb you, sir, but a cholera epidemic is sweeping the city and we are closing the hotel down.'

Von A: 'Last call for dinner? Well, I don't feel so hungry this evening, and anyway I'm expecting a caller.'

Lovely shots of Venice, empty. End of Mahler's Ninth. Click of autochanger. Start of Mahler's Tenth. (Memo to research department: did Mahler write a Tenth?)

Two weeks pass. Von Aschenbecker is in bed, not looking himself.

Von A: 'The service here is getting worse and worse. That's a week since anyone answered the bell. And now I'm dying of cholera. What a great holiday. Maybe it's just as well Tadzio didn't call, because I'm not exactly looking my best.'

There is a knock at the door. He does not hear it. He dies of cholera. Mahler's Eleventh swells up on the soundtrack or, if he didn't write eleven, Brückner's First. The End. (Our grateful thanks to the owners of the Paddington Basin, where most of this film was shot.)

THE MOREOVER ADVICE SERVICE

Problem Corner
Some readers' inquiries
answered

How many Cinque Ports are there?—Nick B. of Lumley Castle.

There were originally five, but over the years the number has gradually been added to, silted up and accreted until there are now at least 73. The best known Cinque Ports are Rye, Sandwich, Turkey, Cress, Deal, Teak, Box, Walmer, Woolmer, Botham, Willey, Dilley, Dungeness, Lydd, Lympne, Lyllee, Thomson, Hyve, Hoathe, Rhymney, Wellington, Churchill, Menzies, W. H. Smith, Old Hastings, New Hastings, Max Hastings, Folkestone and Winchelsea (change at Ashford).

I have read a lot recently about Chatsworth Poussin, but cannot find the recipe. Can you help me?—Robert P. of Canterbury.

Certainly. Poussin is a well known classical seventeenth-century dish much prized in France but not much known in England (until someone tries to export it to America). Personally, I find Poussin a little bland and unrewarding but it can be quite attractive if cleaned, stretched in a wooden frame and then covered with a thin layer of oil. Leave it in natural heat and light for a couple of hundred years (less in a warm climate) until the surface has gone hard and patterned with tiny cracks throughout. It is then ready.

I have often wondered what the derivation of my surname was, and I wonder if you can throw any light on it?—J. Windowcleaner of Parva Magna, Wilts.

Norman immigrants in the Middle Ages almost always retained the name of the place in Normandy from which they came, but it was usually transcribed into the nearest English equivalent. I would guess that your ancestors came from Vent-aux-Clignières, a delightful spot near Caen which was destroyed in 1945 by the Americans. On the other hand, it is a common Parsee custom in India to name one's self after one's job (eg, the Indian cricketers Contractor and Engineer) and you may just be a Parsee without knowing it. You do not mention in your letter what colour you are; a quick look in the mirror will tell you. Parva Magna, by the way, is the Latin for poor little rich girl.

I read recently that the Coptic Pope has been banned in Egypt. Which label are they on, and how many albums have they made? — First-time caller, Kettering.

They are not a group. He is a religious leader. His records are not available in this country.

For many generations our family has had in its possession a curious old vase, which I enclose. Is it of any value? — J. R. of Durham.

No. It is part of a one-off set made in China in the fifteenth century, and so unsuccessful that they never made any more like it. To prevent it cluttering up your home, I will hang on to it and send back instead a lustrous royal wedding platter, personally signed by the deliverer of the 1981 Dimbleby Lecture and due to become a collector's item.

Is there any known cure for Rubik's Cube? — David B. of SE22.

No.

Mrs Thatcher is due to make an important policy speech this weekend on the subject of autumn. Here is an exclusive preview of the text:

AS YOU all know, Britain is going through a difficult period in its history. And as if things weren't bad enough, it now seems certain that in the months ahead we shall be going through what we monetarists call an autumnal period of falling growth. It has begun to happen already. Our party experts have confirmed that the average temperature level is declining, and that there is a fall in the daily availability of light.

Above all, there will be a sharp cutback in the available amount of leaves. In recent months we have been enjoying a boom period of leaves, which have been plentiful, green and big. This is going to change. Owing to world factors beyond our control the leafy times through which we have been passing are going to come to an end for a while. This is not something which is just happening in Britain—there will be a very restricted leaf supply in the whole of Europe—but this does not make the situation any less serious.

I must also warn you that before the leaf shortage comes into effect the economy will be temporarily flooded with a passing glut of leaves, though of a very inferior brown quality. It seems quite likely that this will cause industrial problems such as blocked drains, serious cancellations in rail services and considerable delays on the roads. My experts tell me that this is more likely to happen in the country than the towns, as there is considerable evidence to link the leaf problem with the presence of large numbers of trees.

Now my Government has no intention of being panicked into emergency measures. There are some political leaders in this country who would order government handouts of leaves to pensioners, or spend billions of public money on trying to stick leaves back on trees. I am not one of them.

We must face facts; the fact is that there will be a drop in the natural leaf supply and we must learn to live with it. Those who will be hit hardest by an autumnal cycle—landscape artists, farmers, gardeners, tree surgeons and the like—must simply learn to be *more* efficient, *more* industrious and *more* cost-conscious.

When 1982 comes and people start grumbling that there aren't enough leaves to make compost with or that Britain doesn't look as green as it used to, for heaven's sake remember that we all have to live with it and that you were warned in plenty of time.

My policy is quite clear. There are natural rules governing the supply of leaves in a free market, and to make artificial leaves or to import vast quantities of cheap foreign leaves would be to undermine all that my Government has worked for. If we are patient, I believe that this autumnal cycle will come to an end in six months, perhaps even sooner, and that we could enjoy what we monetarists call a vernal period of regrowth. *This can happen only if we all pull together.*

To say, as some of my opponents do, that we are entering a new Ice Age caused by Conservative policies is folly of the highest order. There *are* leafier times ahead. I believe that 1982 could be a good, green year for *all* of us. But it depends vitally on our not losing our nerve *now*.

Stay with the Tories for a boskier future. Life will be greener, I promise you. Thank you. Good night.

'I WAS cut off, I'm afraid, so I dialled you back, but now we're getting a crossed line. I think I'll ring off and write you a letter.'

Baffled? Can't make head or tail of it? That shows you're not one of the millions of people who have got hooked on to Citizen

Phoning, a new fad with its own private jargon. All you need is a small black 'telephone'; by using its numbered dial you can plug into anyone else in the country who has a similar device. Adrian Wardour-Street, PR man for Citizen Phoning, thinks it's absolutely great.

'I've got to meet so many new people through Citizen Phoning, or STD as we phone people call it,' he explained to me in his office, a phone box in Leicester Square. 'Look, you just dial a number of a friend and you might get through to anyone! Similarly, you often get phoned out of the blue by total strangers, usually wanting to know if Jim is there or speaking Spanish. Well, that breaks the ice immediately and you're off on a new friendship! It's even better with a crossed line.'

Crossed line?

'Well it's a bit technical, but it's a device for allowing a third person to listen to, or even join in with, a conversation between two other people. British Telecom were the pioneers of this one. It really gives you an insight into life. I mean, the other day I tuned into a husband begging his wife to come back, and I was able to join in as a kind of marriage counsellor.'

Did it work?

'It depends how you look at it. I arranged to meet the wife and now we've got a good thing going.'

The jargon used by STD people seems to cover every eventuality. For instance, 'I'll give you a ring sometime' means 'You won't be hearing from me'. 'Mr Jones is in conference' means 'Mr Jones is hiding in the loo till you've rung off'. 'I've got a call from Mr Jones for you' simply means 'My boss, Mr Jones, is capable of many things in life, but dialling a phone call with his own fingers is not one of them'. And if someone should say to you 'Sorry, wrong number', all he means is 'I was thinking of coming round to burgle your house, but I won't if you're in'.

'Some people are so hooked on the whole thing,' says Adrian, 'that they've even had phones installed in their car. You've probably seen them, steering with their elbows. Oh, hold on, that's for me.'

As he spoke, the phone had rung in our Leicester Square box. Adrian answered it.

'Yes,' he said, 'yes, I'll agree to pay for a transferred charge call from New York.' He put his hand over the receiver and winked at me. 'I'll explain later,' he whispered.

THE MOREOVER ADVICE SERVICE

Your Legal Queries
A Lawyer Writes

I thought that all Cabinet minutes could be released after 30 years, so why have they held on to the potentially embarrassing ones about Burgess and Maclean?

The legal position is quite clear on this. Under the Potentially Embarrassing Bits Act of 1976 Cabinet documents may be kept secret if it is in the public interest.

What does that mean—in the public interest?

A thing is in the public interest if it is thought best that the public should not know about it. The legal position is quite clear about this.

Under what Act?

I am afraid it would not be in the public interest to tell you that.

But who would it embarrass now if we learnt about Burgess and Maclean?

More people than you might imagine. Kim Philby for a start.

Surely it doesn't matter about embarrassing Kim Philby?

Not really, I suppose, although he was pretty high up and well respected, you know, and I always got on with him tremendously well. But once you start embarrassing a proven British agent living in Moscow, then it's on the cards that you might start embarrassing unproven British agents living quietly in retirement in Dorking.

Why Dorking?

Nice little place, in the country but near London, good reception from Moscow.

No. I mean, who are you thinking of, living in Dorking?

Under the Mastermind Act of 1972, I pass on that one.

Why are modern Cabinet ministers allowed to reveal Cabinet secrets as and when they happen?

Ah, that's quite different. Under the Accidental On Purpose Leak Act of 1969 the legal position is quite clear, that any Cabinet minister may reveal anything going on in the Cabinet at any time, as long as it is for the purpose of embarrassing the Prime Minister.

Isn't that rather hypocritical?

Certainly. But we don't call it that.

What do we call it?

The British political process.

L IKE EVERYONE else, I have spent the past few years putting together my list of the world's most fabulous women. Unfortunately, my photographs are still away at the secret laboratories to which my local Asian chemist sends everything, but here are my notes on the 10 most beautiful.

Sophie Aubergine. This wonderful French model has a facial bone structure as fine as a filleted kipper. I first saw her face on a French poster in Paris in 1972, and there and then I had to tear it down off the hoarding and bring it home. As it was 20ft × 15ft I had to pay £67 in excess baggage fees, but no matter.

Countess Melanie von Schusnigg. Who now remembers the Munich beauty who was married to Peter Sellers for three days in 1969? I cut her picture out of the paper at the time and have since lost it, but have never forgotten those stripy eyes, as cool as two Everton mints.

Doris. I never learnt her other name. We met in a pub in Leeds in 1975. I asked her for a pint of best bitter. She said: 'Coming up, love.' We never spoke again, but I shall always remember that nose, like a slice of lemon in a glass of advokaat. Oh Doris! Did I leave a pair of gloves on the bar, by the way?

Mrs Patel. In the last lot of prints I received from my Asian chemist there was a picture of a smouldering oriental beauty, with a red beauty spot on her face like an art gallery's already sold sticker on a painting. 'Who can this be?' I said wonderingly. 'It is my wife,' said the chemist, snatching it back.

Wanda Feliskova. The Russian pianist. I have never seen her perform, but on the back of a prized LP of Mozart piano music there is a picture of this wonderful young/old face, with a bone structure like a rondo, wearing a white wig and a high red jacket. I have since learnt that it is a picture of Mozart; but no matter. Feliskova will always be beautiful to me, whatever she looks like.

Carmen Pisco del Almuerzo. Carmen is the Angela Rippon of Peruvian television and I was fortunate enough to see her reading the news once or twice on a fleeting visit last year. Peruvian television does not yet have autocue and she reads from a script on her lap, so it is the top of her head I remember best, but occasionally at the end of sentences she gave me a flashing smile, then got her head down again. Some of our newsreaders would do well to copy her.

Miss Herne Bay (19th). I cannot remember now how I got involved in judging a beauty competition—a lucky deckchair ticket, I think—but I shall always remember the eyebrows of the girl in the Spurs supporters swimsuit, whom I voted for all through. She came last, probably because she said her great ambition in life was to get out of Herne Bay.

Ilse Koenig. An employee of Lufthansa whom I knew briefly in 1979. Not beautiful in the conventional sense, with no figure to speak of, and not gifted with any particular allure, she certainly knew how to retrieve a missing suitcase. Could Sophia Loren or Brigitte Bardot do the same? Thanks, Ilse, and keep the Jack Higgins if it ever turns up.

Patrick Lichfield Not strictly a woman, of course—in fact, not a woman in any sense at all—but it's difficult to see how one can draw up any list without including him. Has anyone ever worn a raincoat better?

The girl in the bus queue this morning. Sensational features, with that sort of soft luminosity that goes beyond mere physical looks. I explained to her that I was doing a list of the world's 10 most beautiful women and that as I was one short would she care to take part at short notice? She hit me and jumped on to a 27. In all my experience of women I do not think I have ever encountered a right hook so soft yet so compelling.

D ID YOU know that the secret of making pasta was lost with the Romans and has never been rediscovered?

That despite this more than 500,000 miles of pasta is produced and consumed *every day* in Italy, at an average speed of 58.6 kpm?

And that Italians can buy pasta in more than 800 different shapes, including butterflies, bow-ties, cog-wheels, ribbons, cuff-links, false teeth, carburettors, mice, fluff, pipe-cleaners, prewar copies of *Oggi*, the staircase of La Scala, the forbidden drawings of Pompeii and roller skates?

Now, you can learn all this and more in Part One of *Pasta!*, a new part-publication on sale today!

Pasta is the simple material which is the basis of so many of the best things in Italian life, like spaghetti, macaroni and the Coliseum. But you don't have to be Italian, because thanks to *Pasta!* it will now take you only 10 seconds to make such delicacies as:—

Sapristi. One of the great side-dishes of Italian history, it is made from equal measures of pasta and Tuscan terra cotta. Left overnight in a kiln, it is ready after a few hours' cooling. When you chew one of these baked morsels, you will say to yourself: 'Sapristi!' (whence, of course, the name).

Marconi. Little round blobs of pasta made into star shapes and worn on the jacket instead of decorations at informal gatherings.

Ferlinghetti. Long, thin strips of pasta which are traditionally flown from rooftops during ceremonial fly-pasts of the Italian Air Force, and in many places have replaced aeroplanes altogether.

With easy-to-follow, step-by-step illustrations, *Pasta!* shows you how to stuff this versatile product into cracks in the wall, use it to weather-proof window frames and do a thousand-and-one tasks around the house. But we also take you back into the first pages of history, six million years ago, when immense deposits of pasta were laid in prehistoric lakes to form stiff and unbreakable layers, as lasagna is made to this very day in so many English restaurants.

Basil and Marjoram are just two of the exquisite writers who will be telling you how you can use pasta, or make it yourself from durum flour. Durum means 'hard' and is pronounced the same as Durham, the jewel of Norman art which lies on an escarpment overlooking the River Wear, which was so eloquently described in *Cathedral!*, last week's new publication, of which a few copies are still left.

Working with pasta will bring you a contentment and peace of mind you thought impossible in the hurly burly of today's busy world. This ancient art of Italian relaxation, part philosophy, part therapy, will unlock areas of your mind you didn't even know existed, will give you a new awareness of family relationships and open your eyes to new things you can get up to with your partner. Although conceived of more as a sport than a martial art, pasta will also allow the single woman to defend herself successfully against any attack late at night, and can be made into the most beautiful jewelry at a fraction of shop costs.

You can't afford to be without *Pasta!* And as an added inducement to buy this 36-part publication, we are giving away with the first number *all the other 35 instalments.*

Get *Pasta!* today and live!

NEXT WEEK at last we can see the first instalment of the most expensive television serial ever made, *Borgialand Revisited.* It cost over £100m to make, or more than the annual budget of Paraguay. But right from the moment producer Shivas Regal decided to film Evelyn Waugh's sprawling historical novel, he knew it was going to be expensive.

'The initial cost was small, just £1.50 to buy a copy of the book in paperback and read it through. But things are never that simple in television and I had to send out a book-buyer to get it, accompanied by a union crew of assistant book-buyer and second unit book-carrier.

'They had to have a hire car, of course, plus eating and emergency accommodation allowance, so at the end of the first day we'd already spent £230 just getting the book from W. H. Smith's. I realized then that it was going to go over budget, especially when I got home and found I had a copy already.

'There have been times, I admit, when I was tempted to give it all up and go and do something simple, like run Paraguay. But in the end it's all been worth it.'

Waugh's classic saga tells the story of a gilded Italian family living quietly in the Roman countryside and becoming so decadent that one of them finally drifts into being Pope. It's told through the eyes of Simon Thrupp, a second-year domestic science student at Oxford, who goes out one summer vacation to stay with the family and teach cooking to their beautiful daughter Lucrezia.

He falls under the spell of the family and when he reappears at Oxford for the 1490 Michaelmas Term, sipping Campari and cooking tomato sauce in his digs, his friends realize that this is not the Thrupp of old.

He then receives a message from Italy: 'Come quickly; Sebastiano ill; Lucrezia affianced; Roberto stabbed; Rodrigo to be Pope; Umberto in foul temper; much cooking to be done—come at once!' He leaves, knowing that life will never be the same again.

'There were lots of problems,' sighs Regal. 'One was that tomatoes had not yet reached Italy. Another was trying to make plausible the relationship between a grand, Old Catholic family like the Borgias, and a student like Simon, who is basically more interested in student grants and following Lancashire's fortunes in the Wars of the Roses. But we got round all these problems by spending more and more on the sets and costumes.'

Jeremy Jeremy, who plays the part of Thrupp, admits that he came to the role with misgivings. 'To me, Thrupp was just a name, a vague character who had something to do with cooking for the Borgias. I now realize he was a towering historical figure who almost single-handed transformed papal banquets overnight from indigestible marathons to light, palatable suppers.

'All that legend about poisoning was merely rumour put about out of resentment at seeing an English cook do so well. I play Thrupp as a sort of medieval Clement Freud; quiet, brooding but with a smouldering majesty.'

The whole epic is lent enchantment and a golden nostalgia by our knowledge that the discovery of America was just around the corner and that the world of the Borgias would be utterly swept away in 400 years by the invasion of hamburgers, Chicago-style pizzas and root beer.

Renaissance Italy has never seemed quite so magical as it does in *Borgialand Revisited*. Of course, Waugh's portrayal of the Borgias as an effete family sitting around studying the latest Leonardo cartoon or popping up to Rome for a party is not the generally accepted vision, but it works beautifully on film and gives logic to the last sad scene as Simon, now a middle-aged balding mercenary catering officer, finds himself quartered in the old Borgia Palace, which has been turned into a fast take-away rigatoni joint.

The first part of *Borgialand Revisited* will be shown on Tuesday on all channels, and the second part comes with it *free*!

Dear Sir,

I could not help noticing in the otherwise excellent first instalment of *Borgialand Revisited* that the Swiss men-at-arms wore crossed edelweiss embroidered on their tunics. This of course is totally inaccurate historically, as any schoolboy will tell you. Crossed edelweiss was not worn until 1507 and then only by officers above the rank of janitor. May I say that the programme brought back memories of many happy hours serving in the Swiss Home Guard during the war years?

Yours etc,
Otto Threlfall.

Dear Sir,

Although I enjoyed the first instalment of *Borgialand Revisited*, I found that the repeated use of the expression 'spiffing!' grated on me. This is simply not a term that a sixteenth-century Italian would have used. The first authenticated use of the term occurs in Arbuthnot's four-volume work in 1737 on climatology: 'The rain did come absolutely spiffing down', and even there the word is probably corrupt. The scriptwriter was probably confusing the word with the Italian adjective 'spiffante', which simply means frothy, referring to hot drinks.

May I say that the programme brought back memories of my years in Italy, when I had the good fortune to be short-listed as the next Pope? Unfortunately, I failed the medical.

Yours etc,
Luigi Cantini.

Dear Sir,

I happened to watch the first instalment of *Borgialand Revisited* and was intrigued to note a character called Rodolfo Sforzini, who was pushed out of a window before he had a chance to say a word. I wonder if this would be the same Rodolfo 'Basher' Sforzini with whom I served in the Swiss Catering Corps in the Vatican in the 1950s? He served the best *cappucchino* I have ever tasted. Unfortunately I was cashiered in 1957 for putting rum in the papal hot chocolate, and we have not kept in touch since.

Yours etc,
Bernard Griffiths.

Dear Sir,

I could not help noticing in *Borgialand Revisited* that Jeremy Jeremy takes a short ride on a red No 34 bus from Ealing to Mayfair. This of course is totally inaccurate, as in 1493 there was no such thing as a red 34. The so-called 'Sketch of a red 34' by Leonardo da Vinci has been proved beyond all doubt to be a troop-carrier for the Swiss Guards.

May I say that the programme brought back many happy memories, though as my wife might read this letter I would rather not say of what.

Yours etc,
Reginald Purblind.

Dear Sir,

Although I enjoyed reading the above letters, may I point out that the practice of signing letters in this newspaper 'yours etc' was dropped in 1934, and that therefore they must be all regarded as unauthentic.

Yours faithfully,
Lord Illegible.

THE MOROEVER ADVICE SERVICE

**Your Money and You
A Financial Expert Answers
Your Queries**

I have heard on TV and else-where that a new world war is likely to break out soon and that one small incident is all it will take to unleash the full horror of nuclear warfare, leaving Europe devastated and our civilization in a state of complete breakdown. What I would like to know is: Will this be likely to affect the value of my antique silver collection?

Almost certainly not. It isn't generally realized that the neutron bomb, beside hurting people more than property, is designed not to damage anything over a hundred years old. This will be a bit hard on people who collect modern art, if you can call it that, but it should have no effect on your silver. It will also clear up a good many problems of authenticity of so-called 'antiques'.

I was among those who sent money to the lifeboat appeal fund in Cornwall, assuming naturally that it would go to help the lawyers and bankers help administer the fund. I now learn that all the money may go to the families, thus adding to their problems and creating an Aberfan dissention type situation, without a penny of it

going to the lawyers. Is there any way I can prevent this happening again?*

Yes. Next time you donate to a worthy appeal, make sure you make your cheque out to 'The Inland Revenue' and send it direct to the tax people.

I am the head of a large industrial group, well-thought of in this country and in 49 others. In fact, I am almost certainly the only person who knows that it is likely to go bust in the next 12 months, costing thousands of jobs and shaking the Stock Exchange. I would very much like a knighthood before then. How do I go about it?

I find it shocking and quite reprehensible that you can bother about a mere title at a time like this. You should be concentrating on salting away large funds overseas. I enclose a copy of my booklet: *The Cayman Islands: Not just a Fun Place.*

I like my mealtimes to be enlivened by a string quartet playing in my small banqueting hall. They have now been with me over a year. Are they tax deductible?

If they are relatives, yes.

Otherwise you can only claim for the value of the instruments, which may be more than the value of the players. If they are foreign players, you should be well off, because you can claim every meal against tax as being entertainment for overseas operatives. There is no need to mention that you are employing your guests.

Acting on the principle that one should buy shares at the bottom as they are bound to go up, I should like to invest in the Polish government. Could you advise me?

Thank goodness that at least one person is approaching the Polish situation in a sane, businesslike way. The Polish generals are making a commendable effort to restore common sense to a disrupted economy, much as the military often do in Latin America. In fact, I think we could get much more perspective on the Polish situation if we treated Poland as a Latin American Country.

Meaning?

Meaning that we ignore it. Anyway, who wants to invest in a *left-wing* general? But if the Poles are serious about their move into a Latin American ambit, I recommend placing a few bob on them in the World Cup.

AT A time when Karpov and Korchnoi are locked in mortal combat on a Swiss hilltop, like two unbalanced characters in a Thomas Mann novel, our thoughts turn naturally to clearing the leaves from the lawn, getting the house double-glazed or indeed anything not connected with chess.

Let me turn your thoughts back against your will to this greatest of all games, back to the days when players did not require personal psychiatrists or yoghurt kits, and revisit with you one of the finest chess matches ever played. It was first published in 1880 and has often been played since, but never so brilliantly as when Droschke, the German past-master, met the flying Hungarian Gobenko in the 1936 Bergen-op-Zoom Tournament.

It is hard to think of two more contrasting players: Gobenko, the excitable Slav with the uncontrollable profile, and Droschke, an incredibly dapper little man— seldom has the chess world seen anyone dapper. They were never to meet again; Droschke rose in the war to become Untergruppenpawnspringer in the Chess Korps, while Gobenko vanished, only to re-emerge in 1947 as a gypsy bandleader with no recollection of his chess career.

The game itself is a perfect example of how cleverly timed sacrifices can lead to crushing victory or, as in this case, utter deadlock.

White, Droschke; Black, Gobenko. Opening—Fool's Stalemate.

1 P-Q4, Resigns!! (An impulsive move by Gobenko, but one which pays off in the ensuing battle for the right flank.)

2 P-Q5, P-Q6. (The more conventional approach is to move one's own pieces, but Black knows what he is up to.)

3 P×P, P×P.

4 P×P, P×P.

5 P×P, P×P.

6 P×P. (Each player is desperately hoping that the other will run out of pawns first.)

6 ....P×P. (If B×Q=4, then BQ+6½=(AB+AC)2, with Black's bishop under pressure.)

7 B-Kt2, 0-0.

8 Q-Kt4, 0-0. (Black has second thoughts about castling.)

9 Q×Q, Q×Q. (For most purposes, both queens are now out of the game.)

10 R-Q1. (Yes, but..)

10 .... Kt-B3. (Yes, but..)

11 P-Kt3. (Oh, well, if you insist. White has now won control of the centre, so much so that he is now in danger of taking his own men. Black now must attempt to find a winning combination.)

11 ......X112X1X2 (with Wrexham v Chelsea as a reserve no-score draw.)

12 Kt-Bt mate!! (A last desperate attempt by the German to save his knight. Gobenko, goaded into fury, resigned and the game dragged on for another five days, though by now the position was hopeless for both sides.)

Answer to last week's problem: Black is awarded the game, because White had placed his king on the wrong square at the beginning.

HERE ARE some recent news stories, only one of which is true. Which one do you think it is?

☐ A recent ring road constructed in the county of Avon unavoidably cut straight through an ancient badger path. After protests by the local preservationists, a small tunnel was built under the ring road at an extra cost of £10,000. But because of the considerable disturbance caused by the contractors, the badgers moved away from the area.

After protests by local preservationists, the authorities then bought a fresh stock of badgers (at some expense) and settled them in so that the tunnel could be used as designed. Unfortunately the new badgers, a slightly different breed, have multiplied fast and are now causing much damage to farms. Local preservationists are demanding that the tunnel be closed.

☐ The Musicians' Union is attempting to unionize birds. Recordings of birds are increasingly being incorporated into performances of avant-garde music, and the union is worried because the birds are neither paid for the job nor union members, yet performing a musical function.

In future they will insist that when bird noises are used the birds concerned *must* receive a reward of some kind, to be agreed by negotiation; or that the noises be made by union members skilled in imitating birds. 'Some of our members have spent long years learning how to sound like a bird,' says the union, 'and we do not intend to stand idly by and see them replaced by a blackleg starling.'

☐ America was not discovered by Columbus or the Vikings, it seems, but by the Chinese. Divers in California have found carved stones under water which are clearly the kind of anchors and block and tackle used by the Chinese 2,000 years ago, remnants of a Chinese shipwreck. Farther off-shore are two more anchors, clearly dropped in panic as the Chinese mariners were driven on to the rocks.

☐ A man in Cumbria has been ordered to knock his house down and rebuild it 10 yards farther away. When checking planning applications, an inspector found that Mr Bob Green's building plans differed from the house he actually built by 10 yards, and although it cost him £35,000 to put up, he must now take it down and reerect it in the agreed place. As the authorities admit that their clerical error was to blame, they are making him a grant of £35,000 to cover the expense.

☐ When Malcolm Griffiths opened a second-hand stamp exchange shop for philatelists in Hendon, he called it SWAPO. He now thinks this was a mistake, as the shop has been burnt down three times in the last year and he is convinced that the South African Secret Service is behind it. 'I had no idea that SWAPO was also the name of an African guerrilla movement,' Malcolm says ruefully. 'Still, it does explain why the Russian Embassy always offered to rebuild the shop for me. When we open again this time, I'll be calling it something different. I'll probably name it after a famous stamp, like the Bermuda Triangle.'

Answer: No 3. The point, though, is which one *you* thought was most likely.

Showbiz—and lots of it!

That's the theme of this year's Royal Showbiz Command Show. And the mastermind behind it is Mr Showbiz himself, Lord Prince.

'I was lying in the bath at the time, smoking quietly and thinking about a theme for the Royal Showbiz show, when suddenly it came to me. Showbiz! I was so excited I dropped my cigar in the water, leapt out of the bath and immediately wrote to 90 of the biggest names in showbiz. Within a week 300 had cabled their acceptance. That's the kind of response you get with the greatest show on earth!'

And what a night it will be.

The greatest acrobats in the world, the Lloyd-Webber family, will be flying across the stage, exchanging cellos in mid-air.

J. R. Ewing's hat will do a sketch with Bob Hope.

Jean-Paul Sartre, Simone de Beauvoir and the legendary Existentialist school will come from Paris to sing: 'Non, je ne regrette l'être et le néant.'

The entire cast of *Nicholas Nickleby* will be flown in from New York just to take a curtain call.

Elaine Page will be flown out to Australia just for the evening.

The best bits from the recent repeats of *Not the Nine O'Clock News* will be shown on a big television set, with the legendary Clive James actually reviewing it on stage!

And the entire history of twentieth-century songwriting will be enacted in dance and mime by the seven writers short-listed for the Booker Prize.

'It's going to be some evening,' says Lord Prince. 'All showbiz will be there. Liza Minnelli, Woody Allen, Ian Botham, Buster Keaton—these are just some of the many people who'd love to be there on the night but can't for one reason or another. I've even had letters from totally unknown people offering out of the blue to star in the show.'

In an effort to accommodate all 128 acts, many of them will take place simultaneously; Lord Prince is especially keen on the prospect of Barbara Woodhouse showing how to house-train the King's Singers.

A squad from the legendary SAS will burst in and rescue Tommy Cooper from his own act.

And Tim Rice will be selling copies of his LPs in the foyer, unaided.

'This is what showbiz is all about,' says Lord Prince. 'An unforgettable evening of star after star. If, at the end of the programme, there is no clear-cut result, we'll go into extra time. And if the whole thing is the success I believe it will be, we'll get them all back again next year.'

A T A time when half the journalists in the world are changing the meaning of words by over-use or misuse, and the other half are writing articles about those changes, I would like to make my contribution to both sides. Here are a few words which I have not seen listed elsewhere.

Confrontation: That dramatic stage in a series of negotiations where both sides refuse to meet the other.

Socialist: A person who is so disgusted by the way power is controlled by a few huge corporations that he proposes to place it in the hands of one giant corporation.

Totally: An adverb meaning quite, moderately, fairly, as in: 'I am totally disgusted by the situation in Peru.'

People: My friends, as in: 'People are totally disgusted by the situation in Peru.'

Taboo: A subject or topic, like cancer or death, that is so sensitive that people talk about it the whole time.

Cinema: A place where you can get a preview of a television film.

Folksinger: A comedian with a guitar slung from his neck.

Opera: A loosely connected series of songs designed to make a full evening's entertainment out of an overture.

Disco: The first ever kind of background music that is louder than anything in the foreground.

Jazz: A kind of music played by blacks and listened to by whites.

Alternative: Normal, fashionable, the way people usually behave.

Domestic science: An attempt to discover the exact scientific laws which govern cookery. The three basic laws are as follows:
1 The amount of butter thrown away with a used butter paper is exactly the same as the amount found in an unused miniature catering packet of butter.
2 No matter how hard you try to empty a packet of sugar, you can always hear some more inside.

3 When a tap is turned on over a sink full of washing up, there is always a teaspoon directly beneath the flow of water, which creates a fountain effect on to the floor.

Catering: An attempt to do away with cooking altogether.

Self: When used as a prefix, the word self has two opposite meanings:

1 Does all the work for you, as in self-adhesive, self-cleaning;

2 Makes you do all the work, as in self-catering, self-drive, self-hire.

Modern: Any music or art created 50 or more years ago.

Preview: That part of a theatre run which is not affected by bad reviews.

Grant: A sum of money given as a bonus and demanded as a right.

Tip: The same.

THERE WAS a widespread feeling at the time of the American election that President Reagan was a much misunderstood man.

Especially by those who voted for him.

I now join myself with those who say that he is misunderstood.

By everyone.

We are told that Mr Reagan, a few days ago, said that a war in Europe was on the cards, or words to that effect. But has anyone studied his actual words?

I have.

Thanks to the *International Herald Tribune*, which had the courage to print the answers he gave at that press conference, I can tell you today that *nobody* could understand what he had said.

Here, when asked if a nuclear war could ever be limited, is what he actually said.

'I don't honestly know. I think, again, until someplace—all over the world this is being, research going on, to try and find the defensive weapon. There has never been a weapon that someone hasn't, come up with a defence. But it could—and the only defence is, well, you shoot yours and we'll shoot ours.'

That passage is short of logic. But it has a certain strange beauty, the far-off elusive quality that we associate with poetry. And there is the clue. Reagan is a poet. And not just any old poet; he is the reincarnation of e. e. cummings. It only has to be set out properly for the true magic of the passage to come through.

*   *   *

i don't honestly know
i think, again, until
someplace
all over the world
(this is being
research going on
to try and find
the defensive weapon)

there never has been a
weapon
that someone hasn't come
                  defence.
          a
      with
up

(But it could)
and the only defence is
well,
you shoot yours

and
we'll shoot ours.

*   *   *

Gentlemen, the man who wrote that could never declare war. He is a poet, not a fighter. *[This writer would like to acknowledge gratefully the generous artistic support of the CIA.]*

A TERRIFIC breakthrough has been reported from the world of contemporary concert music. A computer has been taught to enjoy listening to it. His name is Grant (after the Arts Council money which made him possible) and he is the brain-child of Huw Stockhouse, composer-in-residence at Milton Keynes.

'We've always got things the wrong way round up to now,' says Huw. 'People have been programming computers to write music for humans to listen to. But writing contemporary music isn't the problem—anyone can do that; it's *enjoying* it that's so difficult.

'And after five years' training, Grant really loves it. You should see his little red lights flicker with delight when I put on some Webern. Look, I'll show you.'

Slipping on a pair of ear-muffs, Huw got out a battered LP of

The Golden Hits of Webern Vol 7, and put it on the turntable. Immediately Grant started jogging up and down in his casing, and producing whirring and clicking noises of rapture. On the small read-out screen appeared the words: 'HOT STUFF! CAN WE HAVE VOL 8 NEXT?'

'Not only does he enjoy it,' Huw shouted above the noise, 'but he can distinguish between different composers. Look, I'll show you.'

He took off the Webern, put on some string music by Sir Michael Tippex and pressed the button marked Composer Identification Control. After a while the following message slowly appeared. 'British. Strings. By Elgar. Out of Tchaikovsky. Could Be Anyone. Let's Have the Webern Again.'

'Yes, well, his manners are not of the best,' Huw admitted. 'Normally, if he doesn't like a piece he will adopt the usual language of people unwilling to admit that they hate it—you know, "interesting textures", "swirling clouds of sound" and all that rubbish—but I think he's showing off for you.

'One of his favourites is Kurt Weill, though he tends to think that anything with trumpets and drums, sounding a bit jokey, is Weill. School of National Theatre background music, he calls it.

'Look, let's try an experiement. Here's an LP he's never heard before, some Aaron Copland. Let's see if he can identify it.'

After a few minutes intent listening, the read-out screen burst into action again. 'Oh Blimey. It's Jolly Hoe-Down Time Again. If It's Not Bleeding Folksy American Composers, It's Bleeding English Composers on Wenlock Edge and down Tintagel Way. Carry On Up The Paradise Garden. Knock it Off, Huw. Give Us the Hard Stuff.'

'Gosh, he's in a bit of a mood today', said Huw. 'Right, I'll give him something really hard. A World Premiere off Radio 3. World Derniere, he calls them, when he's feeling low.

'Actually, he hasn't quite mastered the newest stuff. He has a theory that it's now quite difficult to distinguish between the names of composers and the names of compositions. 3 Xenakis by Berio, is one of his little jokes. And Stockhausen No 2 by Boulez.

'He insists that Dallapiccola is a kind of atonal flute. And he refuses to believe that there isn't a Swedish composer called Ring Modulator.'

The World Premiere clinked, bubbled and hiccoughed onwards, but there was no reaction at all from Grant. Huw leant forward and studied the controls intently. He pressed a knob. The screen read: 'ZZZ.'

'Good God,' said Huw. 'He's dropped off to sleep.'

THE MOREOVER ADVICE SERVICE

THE MAJESTY OF THE LAW
A Lawyer answers your Legal Queries

I recently paid a plumber £36.80 for work which has now proved defective. How do I set about regaining the money or getting him to do it again?

You can take him to a small claims court, but these are very small and hard to find. More usual is to sue him for the money, in which case he will go bankrupt to avoid paying. You could then drag him through the higher courts, as long as you are aware that every time you win he will appeal, and vice versa. If you are not satisfied with the ruling of the House of Lords, I would advise you to go to the European Court of Human Rights. In fact, quite honestly, I'd advise you to go straight there, as they seem to side with the small man. It's in Strasbourg, or The Hague, or somewhere. I'll look out the address, if you're interested. Alternatively, I have a young barrister in my chambers who is short of work, and currently moonlighting as a plumber. Why not get him round to take a look?

As far as I can gather from the papers, selection of newspaper editors is now something to do with act of Parliament. This can't be right, surely, can it?

Everything is something to do with act of Parliament. You can rest assured that if you or I can't dig up an Act relating to editors, or Tube train ticket fares, or lifeboat funds, or jokes about Scotsmen, then the Law Lords can. And if they can't, then Lord Denning can. It's often said that people admire our unwritten constitution; it isn't often remembered that they think our laws should be unwritten as well.

But surely half the countries in places like Africa have instituted a Westminster parliamentary system?

There is a growing school of thought, especially among political philosophers like Tony Benn, Arthur Scargill and Pat Wall, that Westminster is now adopting an African parliamentary system.

Why has there been so much fuss about President Reagan addressing both houses of Parliament?

Many people are afraid he may overturn the Law Lords' decision on Ken Livingstone.

Every time I read about a court case, the events in it seem to have taken place in 1975. Why is this?

There is an unavoidable delay in bringing cases to court, usually because the Law Lords cannot find a relevant law, or because nobody knows what the law means, or because the police are too busy making television programmes. As a result, litigants often die or emigrate or become moonlight plumbers and therefore unavailable, before their cases come to court. But the Government is currently working on a Bill which will make the next of kin liable for any litigation involving their deceased parents, even unto the third or fourth generations.

Doesn't that sound a bit Old Testament — the Ten Commandments and all that?

The Ten Commandments were a very early experiment at legislation — short, clear-cut, unambiguous and universally applicable. They could never stand up in a British court of law. One more question, please, then I have to be out mending a cracked pipe.

What does it mean when it says that legal costs have been awarded to the plaintiff or defendant?

Nothing, really. Legal costs are always awarded to the lawyers.

A MRS Phillips of Aylesbury, who describes her job as 'wife of commuter', has kindly sent me a new British Rail, London Transport publication. It is a single sheet of paper headed 'Message to Travellers' and entitled *Autumn Leaves*. It is basically a message of hope and encouragement to those who ride the leaf-prone line from Baker Street to Amersham, and when I read the opening words 'With this year's leaf-fall nearly with us', I was convinced we were setting off into Betjeman country.

With this year's leaf fall nearly with us,
*   See, parading down the tracks,*
The Chalfont Flyer, bringing Brian
*   Back to tea-time, jam and snacks,*
And by the rails, awaiting leaf fall,
*   Silent rows of plastic sacks.*

68

But it was not to be. The more I read, the more I realized that the co-authors of the sheet (H. Reed and M. Fish, divisional managers of BR and LT) were issuing their own declaration of war. 'London Transport's high pressure water cannon is fitted to the leaf clearing train' ... 'Power sanding equipment has been fitted to a number of diesel units' ... 'London Transport has carried out an extensive tree lopping programme on the most difficult section of the line between Chorleywood and Chalfont, and LT staff will be on hand to collect up any large accumulations of leaves' ... 'A suspension of sand in gel—Sandite—gives effective adhesion for about six hours when spread on the rails ... along the vulnerable Rickmansworth-Amersham section.' Yes you're right—it's Journey's End country ...

ACT ONE: *A dug-out somewhere along the vulnerable Rickmansworth-Amersham salient. The acrid tang of Sandite is in the air, and far off we can hear the crump crump of water cannon. A BR corporal is playing a tune on the mouth organ. It is September Song. Enter Major Fish and Captain Reed.*

Fish: Any other tune but that, corporal.

Reed: God, this is a filthy business. Ten million leaves we must have dealt with this morning, and another ten million have arrived from nowhere this afternoon.

Fish: I wish I could get my hands on the man who thought of Sandite. It's an effective adhesive all right. I just wish it didn't stick the bloody leaves to the rails.

Reed: What do they know about war back in London? How's the wound, by the way?

Fish: What? Oh, the knee. Not too bad, considering I got a direct hit from a cannon.

Reed: Water on the knee's a nasty thing.

ACT TWO: *The same dug-out. The corporal is playing 'Autumn Leaves'.*

Fish: Knock it off, corporal.

Sergeant: Sir, sir! Message just through on the field phone. They've been over-run between Chorleywood and Chalfont.

Fish: But I thought we took all the trees down.

Sergeant: Been a change of wind direction, sir. Blown back all the leaves they took off this morning.

Fish: Right! Call out all available staff! We must do it hand-to-hand if necessary.

Sergeant: No one left, sir. Everyone on a sanding sortie north of Amersham.

Enter a young lieutenant. He staggers and collapses.

69

Reed: What's wrong with young Smithers?

Fish: Leaf-shock, captain.

ACT THREE: *Same as before. Corporal is playing I'll Remember April.*

Fish: Oh, very droll, corporal.

We hear a train passing, slowly.

Reed: The 4.50 to Amersham. Think we should have let it through?

Fish: And speed glum heroes up the line to death.

Reed: Oh, don't exaggerate, Fish. At most they'll be late for the Rotary Club.

Fish: God, this is a filthy business. Remember the Great Leaf Fall of 1979?

Reed: When we tried to set fire to the leaves?

Fish: And succeeded only in burning all the sleepers between here and Chorleywood.

There is a loud explosion.

Fish: What on earth was that?

Sergeant: Another power sander blown up, sir. But we've just heard the 4.50's got through.

Reed: Some good news at last!

Sergeant: Unfortunately, it's got through to Watford.

Fish: God, this is an awful business. Think it'll all be over by Christmas?

The corporal starts playing I Talk to the Trees. Fish whips out a revolver and shoots the harmonica from his lips.

Reed: Steady, Fish, steady.

Fish: Sorry, Reed. It's just that I haven't ... I haven't seen my wife since breakfast, and ...

Reed: I know, old man.

Curtain, Interval. Another twenty-nine acts, all more or less identical.

Forget about Bingo.

Forget about Casino.

The Greatest Games are already in *The Times.*

And so many to choose from!
    Why not turn to our Business pages and play *Stocks and Shares?* It's so simple.

We list as many British companies as we can, with the current price of their 'shares'. (These are little bits of paper which help the company 'perform' better.)

70

You buy as many shares as you like in the company you like the sound of best. £1,000 would be enough to buy a few.

A year later you look in the paper to see if your shares have gone 'up'. Then you can sell them again to make a 'profit'!

Or, if they've gone down, you are entitled to go to the company's annual meeting and 'shout' at the chairman.

Either way, you can't lose!

Or, if that strikes you as too risky, you can turn to our Sports pages and play *Horse Racing.*

Every day we print a list of 'horses' who will be running in races the next day. You choose the one with the prettiest name.

Then you go to a kind of stockbroker called a 'bookie' with the money you were saving up for your holiday, and ask for a 'betting slip'. (This is a small bit of paper which makes a horse run faster.)

If your horse comes in the first three, you get your money back. Plus some of the bookie's!

If it doesn't, you put even more money on more horses, till you win.

You can't lose.

Or you can stay with this page and play the biggest game of all. *The Births, Marriages and Deaths* game.

For instance, if you decide to get married to someone, just tell us your names and *we* will print them for you. Yes, your very own names!

It could be the best thing you've ever done. Or the biggest mistake you've ever made. But that's the whole fun of the game!

And there's only a small entry charge.

But next week *Moreover* introduces the most exciting newest game of all—*Times Poker!*

In this thrilling newspaper version of 5-card stud poker, you will be able to play personally against the Features Editor of *The Times.*

Each of you, starting Monday, will get one card a day, and be able to raise your bet each day. On Friday, you will know if you won or lost.

What makes this game so exciting is that you can win lots of money—or lose it!

You have the thrill of knowing that you could bankrupt *The Times* Features Editor. At the risk of making a small dent in your savings.

If you want to play this greatest of all newspaper games, send your opening stake *now.* Something small to start with. Let's say £100.

The fun begins on Monday. Don't forget—you only get New 5-Card Stud Poker in *The Times!*

Let's see the colour of your money, stranger.

A S MOUNT Everest is becoming one of the most crowded mountains in the world, it may be useful for readers to have a resumé of expeditions which are at present attempting to climb it. Here is a check list of some of the most interesting to cut out and keep:

The White House Feasibility Study Group: A somewhat mysterious team who are building a road up the little-used southwest corner capable of taking trailers and heavy plant. When asked at a press conference if the intention was to place cruise missiles on Everest, President Reagan replied: 'This, at the time we are, is another matter, anyhow.'

Nat West Team B: A volunteer squad of cashiers from the National Westminster Bank are battling their way up the normal route installing night safes every 1,000 feet. The theory is that there will be a great demand for places to deposit the huge sums of sponsorship involved in mountaineering these days. 'In retrospect,' a bank spokesman admits, 'we would have done better to install hot drink machines. But at least we are going to beat Barclays to the top.'

The Mount Everest Marathon: More than 13,000 entries have been received for this, the toughest of all marathons, which starts on November 26 and it is hoped will end the same day.

Japanese Business Week on Everest: The enterprising Japanese are aiming to stage the first trade fair on Everest next month, in three vast inflatable tents which will be flown in by helicopter. They have four weeks in which to find a solution to the fact that helicopters cannot fly that high.

'Game for a Laugh' Outside Broadcast: Independent television are sending the entire production team of this knock-about programme to the top of Everest to film the highest snowball fight in the world. 'Basically we are looking for two things,' a spokesman said. 'One, we are after a bit of a giggle; two, we are hoping they won't come back.'

The All British Trade Union Exhibition: Fierce disputes have so far restricted progress to the establishment of base camp, but leaders are cautiously hoping for gradual progress after all-night talks. One trouble seems to be that some members will climb only on Saturday nights for one shift. Another is the temperature, which many members have totally rejected as being far too low.

The Manchester United Supporters' Expedition: An all-male team of 500 youths in the distinctive scarf and boots, they are at present rampaging around the lower slopes and causing considerable damage. They have little hope of getting to the present top but hope to break up the mountain sufficiently to bring it down to a manageable height.

Lord Lichfield and the Most Beautiful Women in the World: The well known photographer is leading 15 of his favourite models up Everest in an attempt to prove that it can be climbed totally without use of make-up. 'Progress is slow,' he reports, 'but they are absolutely divine to work with and I don't care how long it takes. The light, by the way, is out of this world.'

TIMES READERS have probably noticed a frequent feature in their newspaper called The Times University Results Service.

You may have wondered what The Times University was, and what it offers you.

For those who are seriously interested in enrolling, I would like to explain in a little more detail.

The Times University is a modern building clad in plastic ivy which stands in 15 acres of rolling parkland just off the Grays Inn Road. Here, students may spend up to three years studying all aspects of modern communication. Senior students have their own rooms; most students work in large open-plan study areas, each with his own hot-drink machine, photocopier and telex receiver.

The most popular courses are:

Information Service Theory

This course not only teaches students how to convey the most information in the least space but offers informational philosophy, which is concerned with the relative value of, say, high tide in Ilfracombe and a lecture on herbaceous gardening in Ancient Greece, or the comparative usefulness of the announcement that (a) the A4 is reduced to no lanes (b) the Duke of Kent is going to a football match.

The Theory and Practice of Birthdays

Students are given enough mathematical grounding to work out how old a person is, given his birth date. There is also a series of seminars on the value of announcing a famous person's birthday on the day itself, by which time it is already too late to send him a card, buy him a present or get invited to his party. Case histories are studied of well-known people who would die rather than have their age published.

World Leadership
Students are taught to compose short moral essays known as leaders containing advice which, if taken by world leaders, would bring peace and prosperity in no time.

Advanced Semantics
The study of crosswords. Students can apply for this course only if they already have a good working knowledge of minor Victorian poets, geographical abbreviations and unusual short words.

Supplementary Information
A course on how to put together supplements on interesting areas, especially in the Middle East, and more especially on how to find subjects not so far covered by supplements.

The Arts, Especially Opera
The study of the arts, especially opera.

The Law and Order of Rules
The theory and practice of separating pieces of prose by long thin black lines or short thick ones.

Comparative English Prose
The study of different styles needed in a newspaper. Why, for example, it is all right for a private advertiser to write: 'Flat, W'minster, 2 rms, k & b, own patioette, wd suit bachelor sheikh', but not all right for a parliamentary reporter to write 'Hse of Commons, lge chamber, today, Foot slams Prior over Belfast (2 dead, 1 w'ded) Ayes 298 Noes 234.'

Correspondence Course
A course in correspondence or letter-writing. Students are taught how to choose subjects and adopt approaches which would make their letters more eligible for publication. There are several specialist courses. (1) The 'I was actually there, so I know what happened' school. (2) The 'I am in the Government, so I know what is going to happen' school. (3) The 'I am a local ambassador, and my government would be cross if I did not protest' school. (4) The 'I think it would be fun to start a correspondence on the pros and cons of moustaches' school.

The Reading of Proofs
The art of avoiding mipsrints.

The Great Sea Saga of **Photocopier III**

Reports received from on board Photocopier III, our entry in
The Observer Transatlantic Boat Race.

June 9

Conditions are very difficult at the moment. In these Force 8
winds I find it extremely hard to type, as the motion of the
boat often sends the carriage of the machine to the end of the
line before I have started it. I have rigged up a temporary self-
righting gear for it, but it breaks down two or three times a
day.

I am also doubting the wisdom of taking an electric typewriter with us, as salt crystals are perpetually forming on the
golf ball and I have to stop after every paragraph to remove
them. In addition, the small generator which runs the
typewriter broke down this morning, and only prompt action
by 'Evoe' Knox-Johnston, my crew, got it going again. The
next time I write the day-to-day account of a voyage like this,
I think I shall prefer an old-fashioned manual machine. The
photocopier, though, is working absolutely tremendously and
there have been no problems at all.

The worst problem about a long sea voyage such as this, I
think, is the lack of loneliness. I am constantly being
interrupted by the crew with queries about navigation and the
set of the sails, as they are called. He does not seem to realize
that it is the captain's job to write a lucid, powerful and best-
selling journal of the voyage, not to get bogged down in
details which he is perfectly capable of working out for himself. How can I work out alternatives for clichés like
'towering waves' and 'scudding clouds' if people are always
coming to me with moans about spinnakers being swept
away? Next time I shall have a cabin with a lock.

This morning we sighted a waterlogged copy of a Naomi
James paperback, presumably jettisoned by some other
yacht. We left it in the water.

Two boxes of A4 paper were washed overboard in the night
but the other 92 are safe, thank God. I have given orders for it
to be lashed more firmly, to avoid a repetition of this near-
disaster.

The only craft we sighted today was a Liberian oil tanker going the other way. We tried to hail it in order to get them to take my first two completed chapters back to London, but they did not understand us and failed to stop. Neither of us speaks Liberian, unfortunately. I have given orders for photocopies of the chapters to be thrown overboard in the empty bottles so kindly provided for the purpose by the Scotch industry, in case the unthinkable should happen.

The bundles of last Sunday's *Observer* are safe in the hold, if a little damp. The management presumably knows best, but I cannot help thinking every time I look at them that it's hardly surprising the English Sunday papers get to New York so late.

© Moreover Maritime Enterprises Ltd

June 16

Dawn in the Atlantic is a truly breathtaking spectacle, or so I am informed by my crew, 'Evoe' Knox-Johnston, who is always up at some unearthly hour crashing around on the deck upstairs with brooms and buckets and God knows what. As I have to be up very late in the evening correcting my typescript for my book, *Before Me The Ocean,* I find this totally lacking in any kind of consideration.

Back home in London there is a woman in the flat above me who gets up way before breakfast and makes a terrible racket with her cleaning, which is one of the reasons I came to sea in the first place. To find that even in mid-Atlantic I have the clatter of housework going on upstairs is almost more than I can bear. I am only thankful that 'Evoe' did not bring a vacuum cleaner.

Our morning routine changes little. At about nine Knox-Johnston brings me coffee in bed, and we work out the day's tasks. He looks after what little navigation and sailing there is to be done, while I try to get out of him whether it will be fine enough for me to type in the open, or whether I should stay in bed away from the elements. His forecasting is not always, I am afraid, very reliable.

Yesterday he assured me that it would stay dry until lunch, yet no sooner had he brought me elevenses in the cockpit than it came on to drizzle. Seeing the paper go to shreds as I type is bad enough; being put in mortal danger by sparks from my electric typewriter is altogether something else.

June 17

Today I find a terrible thing has happened. By now we should be entering warmer climes, with flying fish alongside and friendly dolphins basking near by. I asked Knox-Johnston if we would soon be near the Equator. To my amazement he said that not only were we not near the Equator, but that we would go nowhere near it on a trans-atlantic race.

'Transatlantic?' I said. 'But we are going round the world!' He then informed me with ill-concealed satisfaction that we were going no further than North America. I find this news incredible. How can one write a classic of the sea by merely popping across the Atlantic? These days the public will settle for nothing less than a circumnavigation, and by a woman if possible.

I have issued an ultimatum to Knox-Johnston to go right round the world, but he says nothing. I can, however, hear him muttering on deck to himself. I fear I may have a mutiny on my hands.

© Moreover Maritime Enterprises Ltd

June 30

More mechanical trouble to report, I'm afraid. My job as captain—to write a best-selling account of the voyage entitled *Before Me The Ocean*—could not be done satisfactorily without a constant supply of hot coffee, and after much consultation with several lone round-the-world typists, I decided to install a constant percolating machine. I now think that was a mistake. In high winds the coffee slops over the top and burns on the electric element; the resultant noxious smell is hardly disguised by my Gauloises and I am driven up on deck where I am naturally sea-sick. Next time I shall take an electric kettle and big tin of instant.

My crew, 'Evoe' Knox-Johnston, who spends most of the day and night idly at the helm, is a non-smoker. That probably explains why, when courteously asked to empty my ashtray, he tends to throw ash and tray overboard together. Luckily, I found a large brass ashtray screwed to the deck upstairs, which I have taken into my study and keep hidden from him.

Later. An interesting talk with 'Evoe'. It appears that his uncle was Mgr Ronnie Knox-Johnston, a member of the Crazy Gang.

Later still. I am worried about 'Evoe'. He stood behind me for two hours as I typed, then suddenly said: 'There are two r's in coruscating.' I went to look for my dictionary, but it was nowhere to be seen.

July 1

I retrieved a book from the sea which came floating past us. It was my dictionary. I firmly suspect 'Evoe' of having just thrown it overboard, but he denies it utterly. The ocean can do strange things to a man.

Later. Land! At last, after nearly three weeks, we are in sight of the end. The United States is a green, soft place, not at all full of sky-scrapers as I had been led to expect.

Even later. Having put ashore, we accosted a man working in the fields. 'Sure,' he said, 'this is not America at all, at all. This is the Emerald Isle. But keep going west and you can't be missing it.'

I berated 'Evoe' bitterly for his navigation, but he was recalcitrant. How could he be expected to steer straight, he wanted to know, if some idiot had removed the binnacle from the cockpit. I fail to understand what he means, unless he is referring to the simple transfer of a brass ashtray downstairs. I fear this may prove to be a long and arduous journey.

© Moreover Maritime Enterprises Ltd.

July 9

We have been becalmed off Ireland for several days now, so I would imagine that our chances of winning the race, even on handicap, are slim. But the weather is beautiful and the object is not to win but to write a book, so I am not unhappy.

I wish I could say the same for my crew, 'Evoe' Knox-Johnston. We both miss the morning papers very much, I as a writer because it means I have to get straight to work after breakfast, he because he needs the weather forecast and in the absence of a paper has to rely on a short-wave radio. This morning he picked up the news that 'Tiny' Rowland has been allowed to buy *The Observer*. Apparently the Monopolies Commission decided it was all right for him to sponsor *The Observer* Race, which now constitutes virtually the whole British naval deterrent. 'Evoe' is upset because, he says, Lonrho will insist on the Race starting from Africa in future and he is very subject to heat rash. Well, I have never met 'Tiny' Rowland but I am glad for him. Dwarfs have a hard enough time without the Monopolies Commission gunning for them.

'How's the book coming on, Thor Heyerdahl?' said 'Evoe' jokingly this morning. I could have hit him. Heyerdahl and Severin and that lot are not real writers. It's all very well building boats out of rice paper and proving that chefs could have sailed from Hong Kong to London in 1066, but what's the point if you take modern typewriters to write the book?

Of course, I have all the modern aids, but I also have below decks Susie, a goose, who keeps me supplied with quills. Only by using truly authentic writing tools can I prove that Tudor seamen could have written books during their voyage. So far, I have found that in some ways quill and parchment is superior to typewriting. If a wave breaks over a quill, you just shake the water off. If it breaks over the typewriter, you get a blinding flash and 300 volts coursing through you.

Later. 'Evoe' has some very interesting relations. He told me at dinner that he is the nephew of 'Groucho' Knox-Johnston, the wit and prelate. Apparently 'Groucho' was once offered a cardinal's hat but turned it down saying: 'I wouldn't believe in any god who was prepared to forgive me.'

'Evoe' is coming on as a cook. For dinner he served an extremely tasty casserole swimming in garlic and tomato. When I complimented him. he said. 'Yes, usually they're too rich and oily, but this one was fine.'

Later still. I have just realized what he meant. I rushed downstairs, but Susie is no more. I instantly dismissed 'Evoe' from my service, but in mid-Atlantic this is harder than it sounds, and I have reluctantly reinstated him. I fear trouble lies ahead, though.

© Moreover Maritime Enterprises Ltd.

November 10

This is my first dispatch to you since July 9. To those of my readers who had given me up for lost, and to those of my sponsors who had given me up as unviable, may I just say this: I have been held totally incommunicado by my captors.

Yes. You have read correctly. For the last four months I have been in the hands of the Irish Secret Police. You may remember that on July 1, thanks to the total incompetence of my crew 'Evoe' Knox-Johnston, we made landfall on what I hoped would be America but turned out to be Ireland, and were subsequently becalmed just off shore. A quarter of an hour after telephoning to *The Times* another instalment in my forthcoming book *Before Me The Ocean*, I was arrested and taken before two Irish policemen.

'So, it's a spy you are, is it?' said one roughly.

Appalled, I realized that they suspected me of the kind of activity that Russian submarines have recently popularized off Sweden.

'Certainly not,' I said. 'I am a writer aboard *Photocopier III,* sponsored by Wizzamatic the machine that solves *all* your office problems. Why not ask for a free demo...'

'A *writer*, is it?' said the second policeman, cutting short my nautical explanation.

'By God, you're in trouble now. You'll soon wish you were a spy.'

Not ten minutes after he had made a hurried phone call, the door burst open and in walked the man I came to know as Flynn.

'Irish Secret Police,' he said, flashing a badge.

'Begob,' said one of the policemen. 'I never knew we had a Secret Police.'

'Sure,' said the second, 'and what would be the point of having one if people knew about it?'

'Out of here, you two stage Irishmen,' said Flynn angrily. 'Leave me to interrogate this man.'

I thought I would be ready for any kind of interrogation, being a writer and therefore used to lying. One lies mostly to publishers who ring up and ask questions like, 'How is the book coming along' or, 'How do you justify a further advance?' But Flynn put me through an ordeal which called on my deepest resources.

It seems that writers are allowed to live in Ireland tax-free, if permitted to enter. Those not permitted to enter often try to sneak into the country by small boat and go to ground. Flynn thought I was one of those. He therefore put me through a series of tests designed to see if I were a genuine writer or not.

He filled me full of Guinness, with a stopwatch in his hand.

He gave me five new novels and demanded a review within 24 hours.

He took me on all-night literary pub-crawls round Dublin.

He made me give ten reasons why I could have written *Ulysses* better than James Joyce.

He challenged me to get advances from five different publishers for the same book.

He got me to destroy the reputations of ten writers I secretly admired.

And after four months of this non-stop ruthless examination he declared that I would now be permitted to take up residence in Ireland. He was, I think, nonplussed for the first time when I declared that I wanted nothing of the sort and would sail straight on to New York, as soon as they had released Knox-Johnston.

'Oh, your fellow Knox-Johnston has been at liberty all this time,' he said. 'We never suspected him of authorship. He has many relations here, with whom he has been having a rare old time. Apparently his fore-fathers went over on the *Mayflower*.'

'That doesn't explain why he has relations here,' I said icily.

'Apparently they didn't like the look of the place and came straight back.'

So now I am ready to sail on, as soon as 'Evoe' has properly installed the cask of stout his relations insist on giving him. I shall not, I think, now win the race, but what a chapter in my book it will all make! Now for the open sea, at last.

© Moreover Maritime Enterprises Ltd.

April 7

One of the last things you expect to see in the southern Atlantic is a British submarine, so I and my crew, 'Evoe' Knox-Johnston, were taken aback when a huge sub emerged in front of us this morning. We knew it was British because of the Union Jack painted on the conning tower and 'Come On You Spurs!' scrawled on the side.

'I wonder if you could tell us the way to the Falkland Isles?' said the very polite officer who eventually appeared.

'Straight on,' I said.

'*Immer geradeaus,*' said Evoe.

The officer looked very curiously at Evoe. I thought it would take too long to explain that he has been learning German from the BBC World Service, and insisted on speaking nothing else before lunch; anyway, there were more important matters.

'Do you think you could pop over and have a look at our radio?' I said.

'Delighted, old boy.'

The trouble with the radio is that ever since we left Ireland four or five months ago it has been receiving but not trans-mitting, which explains why *Times* readers have not heard from me, nor have been told about our decision to give America a miss and go round the world. There are very few records left to break, and one of them is to be the first boat to go round the world during a transatlantic race.

Everything is going beautifully. The weather is so good that Evoe has given up wearing clothes and goes around with only a huge pair of field-glasses round his neck. He is the only man I know with a bathing suit mark in the middle of his chest.

'What's your business in the Falklands?' I said, when the man had fixed the radio for us. He put his finger to his lips, and looked round to see if anyone was listening.

'Very hush hush,' he said.

People go rather odd when they sign the Official Secrets Act, I find.

'My God, look at that!' he said suddenly. He had just noticed the Spurs graffiti on his sub.

'A bit bad form,' I said.

'It certainly is,' he said furiously. 'I'm a QPR supporter, always have been. Heads will roll for this. Well, goodbye.'

'*Hasta la vista*,' I said. He looked at me curiously before he, and then the sub, vanished. I suppose I ought to have explained that I have been learning Spanish from the BBC World Services. Evoe and I sometimes have long chats without a single word of English appearing.

'*Entonces*,' I said, 'let's make for the Falkland Isles and do some restocking. It'll be nice to spend an hour or two on shore in absolute peace and quiet. The Falklands must be the most off-the-beaten-track place possible for an undisturbed weekend. OK, *amigo*?'

'*Ausgezeichnet*,' says Evoe.

Our next report will be from the sleepy Falklands, then. *Hasta luego, mis lectors amados*!

© Moreover Maritime Enterprises Ltd.

April 14

I wish someone would explain to me what is going on.

As I reported last week, we had intended to put in at the Falkland Islands for a quiet weekend. There is nowhere quieter in the world than the Falklands, unless perhaps it's the

Foreign Office at weekends, or so I was once told by a friend who works at the Foreign Office at weekends. (He works in the section which is trying to phase out what's left of the Empire—he himself is in charge of getting rid of the Falklands, though he says it's a hopeless task.)

Anyway, I was bowling along through the south Atlantic yesterday—my crew 'Evoe' Knox-Johnston, has the technical details if you're interested—when a huge aircraft carrier came out of nowhere, towards us. I was idly watching it through binoculars when to my amazement a plane took off from it, circled towards us and peppered the sea around us with what I can only imagine were bullets.

'What on earth was that?' said Evoe popping up from downstairs, where he'd been poring over what he calls charts, though they look just like maps to me.

'We're being attacked,' I said. 'Stand by to repel jet fighter aircraft.'

'Oh ha, bloody ha,' said Evoe. Then the plane did another sweep over us.

'I take it all back,' said Evoe. 'What do we do now?'

'As captain of this vessel,' I said importantly, 'I order you to take over and do what you think fit.'

Evoe immediately changed course to head straight for the aircraft carrier, explaining that the safest place is right next to it, where they can't attack you and often can't even see you. Soon we were close enough to see that it was called *Invincible,* which I guessed from my World Service Spanish lessons was Spanish for invincible. It was clearly an Argentinian ship.

'Leave this to me, Evoe,' I said, and in my best Spanish I announced through the loud-hailer that steam gives way to sail, and would he kindly move over. Somewhat to my surprise, we were answered in British through what sounded like a 20-ton disco system: 'This is a Battle Zone—Kindly Keep 200 Miles From Port Stanley!'

Five minutes later the ship was a smoking dot on the horizon, and we two, rather shaken, were discussing what it all might mean. Evoe was sure it was a British ship but I have a friend who works in the Admiralty at weekends, in the section which is trying to phase out the Navy, and I am sure we have nothing that big left.

'Well, somebody is at war with somebody, that's for sure, and we're in the middle of it,' said Evoe. 'If you ask me, Britain and Argentina are fighting each other, and that can mean only one thing: the World Cup has started.'

'There'll be trouble in the Middle East, mark my words,' I said. 'I have a friend who works in the Israeli army at weekends, and he says that whenever there's a big international hoo-ha such as Poland or Afghanistan, they always undertake some unnoticed offensive.'

'That, if I may say so, is neither here nor there. Look, the next ship that comes may take offence at being addressed in either Spanish or English, so let me use my German, OK?'

'How many Argentinians understand German, for heaven's sake?'

'More than you might think,' said Evoe mysteriously.

He got his chance sooner than we expected. Not two hours later a submarine surfaced silently beside us and three officers emerged on deck, though whether British or Latin American I could not tell. Evoe shouted to them in his best German that we came in peace, that we were unarmed and that nuclear power gave way to sail. The officers conferred, and then shouted back something also in German.

'Oh my God,' groaned Evoe. 'Sometimes I wish I'd never learned German.'

'Why, for heaven's sake?'

'It's an Israeli sub,' said Evoe. 'Apparently the war isn't hotting up as they'd like, and they've been sent to cause an incident.'

'What sort of incident?'

'As far as I can gather, they intend to blast us out of the water.'

I will relate the sequel to all this in my next dispatch. Meanwhile, as I think I may have said already, I wish someone would explain to me what is going on.

© Moreover Maritime Enterprises Ltd.

L EGAL HISTORY was made yesterday when a male defendant pleaded guilty but menopausal. Here is an extract from the trial.

Defence counsel: The charges against my client are basically, my Lord, that he did defraud his employers of £1,500,000 over three years. He admits that he did this, or seems to remember doing this, but must point out that he was driven to it by a serious mid-life crisis.

Judge: A what?

Counsel: Just as women are driven to wild deeds by premenstrual tension, and subsequently are released by the courts, so men suffer in their forties from mid-life crisis, which forces them out of their normal behaviour.

Judge: Three years seems a long time for a bit of impulse fraud.

Counsel: The crisis lasts that long, my Lord. Also, it takes that long to salt away £1.5m.

Judge: Good point. But what is this crisis like?

Counsel: The symptoms are despair over the direction of one's life, worry over one's physical make-up, a sense of alienation from loved ones and a deep conviction that one will never be attractive to girls.

Judge: Sounds like adolescence to me.

Counsel: It is very like adolescence, but without the craving for loud music.

Judge: Well, I don't remember this happening to me in my forties.

Counsel: Nor do I. But science has now established that lawyers have a different life cycle from other humans, and we reach the stage of contemplative old age in our mid-twenties. Lawyers do not have to worry over the direction of their lives.

Judge: Hmm. Does the defendant have a loyal and trusting wife who is prepared to stick by him through thick and thin? It is normal in these cases, I believe.

Counsel: His wife insists on staying with him to help save the marriage. That, of course, puts him under even greater stress.

Judge: Is there another woman?

Counsel: No, my Lord, I am happily married.

Judge: Good. So your client committed fraud because he felt a bit unhappy?

Counsel: He was driven to fraud by a chemical imbalance which deranged his judgment temporarily. Also, he was a bit short of the ready.

Judge: And you are asking me to believe that this is a peculiarly male illness?

Counsel: I propose to call fifty expert witnesses to testify that man's instinct as a hunter, a provider and a senior member of the tribe is severely damaged by society today.

Judge: I have never felt an urge to go out and fill little birds with bits of metal.

Counsel: I would guess that your Lordship's instincts are wholly channelled into being a wise sage of the tribe.

Judge: I see that one of your witnesses is George Melly. I thought he only appeared in cases concerning obscenity or the Surrealist school of painting?

Counsel: Normally, yes. But I think you will find it hard to resist his rendition of 'Nobody knows you when you're down and out'.

Judge: Your client can hardly be said to be down and out. If I find him innocent, as I am strongly tempted to, how do we know he won't go out and have another crisis?

Counsel: My client is now cured, my Lord. He has formed a deep and lasting relationship with the £1.5m, and that has restored him to normality.

Judge: Good. I like a happy ending. Right, on with the show!

The trial continues.

YOU'VE HEARD of *la nouvelle cuisine*. Now comes *nouveau gourmet writing*! This is an exciting new style of cookery writing which does away with the old dry-as-dust traditional clichés and makes each recipe seem a thrilling challenge.

Normal cookery methods seek to reduce difficult dishes to a prosaic level, within reach of everyone. *Nouveau gourmet writing* takes simple recipes and tries to make them sound impossibly complicated, giving them a richness and intricacy you'd never dreamt they possessed. If you've ever been stumped by a recipe, it was *nouveau gourmet*.

Today Moreover Publications present the first in a series of new approaches to familiar dishes.

Cheese and Lettuce Sandwich

1 lettuce
3 slices cheese
2 slices bread

Choosing a lettuce is something that is often done in a hurry, but the conscientious sandwich-maker knows that the wrong leaf can

87

often ruin a promising sandwich. It is no use, for instance, using a Cos lettuce leaf for a dainty squared sandwich, as the leaf will project five or six inches out of the sandwich and confuse drivers behind who will think you are turning right.

Again, there are many attractive crinkly lettuces on the market, like green Afro-hairdoes, but these should be used in sandwiches with extreme caution; there is nothing more embarrassing than unpacking a sandwich and seeing the top fly yards into the air as the pressure is suddenly released.

I'd recommend a Webb's Wonder for safety or an iceberg for economy, as long as you remember to take the plastic bag off the latter.

A lettuce should be wiped rather than washed. Some experts favour putting water into the bag in which the lettuce comes, plus a little green washing-up liquid, then shaking vigorously. I demur. Much better to give each leaf an individual wipe with a clean chamois leather, then bring to a fine viridescent shine with a dry cloth. Or tumble dry for five minutes at 20C, taking care not to mix with white shirts or colour-run jeans.

Once chosen and cleansed, a lettuce must be reduced to the size of the putative sandwich. For some years it has been fashionable to say that lettuce leaves should always be torn, not cut, but something in my bones tells me it's time for a change.

So take a knife (a good quality French stainless steel knife, not a shoddy English department store utensil or the No 12 attachment on your Swiss Catering Corps gadget) and fillet the leaf as they do in Szechuan cookery, discarding the ribs and veins and keeping only the fleshy part, rich in water and chlorophyll. (See diagrams 1–10.)

The lettuce will now have to be kept in prime condition while you go out and select the right cheese from your local cheese-monger.

The peasants of northern Bulgaria keep lettuce leaves for days on end stacked under the weight of a heavy stone on a south-facing hillside, which is marvellous for preserving their shape. As it turns them brown and mildewed, I would not recommend this method; instead, pop them in a plastic bag and put them in the salad drawer of your fridge, or, if you have not got a fridge, the Holiday bookings folder of your filing system.

Meanwhile, you are left with the lettuce root, or should be. If you are loth to discard it, it makes a very good lettuce-root stock simmered for an hour with bayleaf, onion and chamois leather.

Lettuce-root broth is much prized by the Laplanders during the long winter vigil over their reindeer herds; either turn your stock into lettuce broth or send your lettuce roots direct to Oxfam, Box H51A, Helsinki, Finland.

So much for the lettuce. Now for the cheese.

(From guest columnist Anna Paukenschlag, of the Very Angry Indeed Women's Press.)

CHRISTMAS IS, in a very real sense, a woman's festival. That the baby Jesus played a substantial part in the historic event we know as Christmas cannot be denied, but his time was still to come. If Christmas belongs to anyone, it belongs to Mary—the mother, the woman, the person on whom in fact all the responsibility fell, as it so often does.

If this comes as a surprise or even a shock, it is for the very simple reason that all the surviving accounts of Christmas were written by men. The male-oriented gospels of Matthew, Mark, Luke and John very naturally give a patriarchal view of the events at Bethlehem; it never even occurs to them to think of the shepherds' wives who were deprived of a sight of the Messiah, or even of the three wise women patiently waiting for their menfolk to return from their pursuit of the Star in the West (as it must have seemed to them).

But the main victim of this blinkered male approach has always been Mary. She is allowed a role as a recipient of a visit from the Holy Ghost, and the mother of the babe, but this has always struck me as verging on the Mills and Boon. The element of romance has always covered up the fact that Mary was a disadvantaged mother in a homeless situation, forced to embark on the most fulfilling experience of her life in sub-standard lodgings, surrounded by farm animals and all the risk of disease that that implies. It was typical of a fascist government like the Roman colonialist empire that she should be forced to travel far from her home simply for bureaucratic convenience.

Of course her husband was there as well. I do not deny that. As men go, Joseph seems to have been comparatively aware and caring. But then, he could afford to be. He had a fulfilling job as a carpenter, he was in employment, he had a wife to attend to his every want. Mary, on the other hand, was caught in the classic wife-of-a-working-man situation; no job of her own, forced to stay in the stable all day, no independent life and with an unplanned pregnancy on top of everything.

89

Honestly, nothing seems to change, does it? It really makes you furious. And if somebody had to cook Christmas lunch 1981 years ago, you can bet your bottom dollar it wasn't Joseph. And do we find any women among the twelve disciples? Or any women writers penning letters to the Ephesians? We most certainly do not. All that women are allowed to do in the New Testament is have babies and stand around comforting the menfolk. It makes me so mad. I mean, if Christianity can't take the lead, who can?

We *must* wake up to the enormous conspiracy against women spelt out so clearly in the Bible. I am not saying that God himself is a male chauvinist. Well, yes I *am* saying that God is a male chauvinist. What else do you expect? God has a satisfying job creating the world, no money problems, top social position. how could he possibly understand women's problems?

Honestly, it makes me so cross I can't go on.

Next week: Christmas—a Zen Buddhist view.

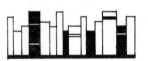

I THINK I detect a new fashion.

The flood of books beginning with the word 'Not' may be on the ebb.

And they may just be replaced by books, programmes and films with titles like *Did Darwin Get it Wrong?*

A well-known publisher said to me the other day: 'For heaven's sake don't blab it to *Times* readers, but there's a fortune to be made in doubts about evolution.'

One man who agrees is 'Cocker' Leakey, the brilliant but blunt Cockney paleontologist who gave up his taxi-driving job in 1967 when a passenger left a bag of bones on the back seat. Cocker sat up all night trying to piece them together, and though they were later reclaimed by the police for an important case, the bug had bitten him. He now has a successful television series, *If the Bone Fits*, and a book in the best-seller list, *Not just a Pretty Skull*.

But he reckons his next book, *Did Darwin get it Upside Down?* will be the blockbuster to really make his name.

'Bit of a split infinitive in that last sentence, squire,' twinkled Cocker as we sat together in his local, the Skull and Trowel. 'Offends my rough proletarian sensibilities, if you don't mind my saying so. Now, what was it you wanted to talk about?'

'Well, a well-known publisher was telling me the other day that you think you can disprove evolution.'

'Blimey, well-known publishers never get it right, do they? Beats me how they ever get well known. No, evolution is all right as far as it goes. It's just that, way I see it, Darwin got things the wrong way round.'

'Meaning, it's the survival of the unfittest?'

'Well, there is something in that. I mean, if butterflies flew in a straight line like it's only sensible, they'd all be extinct by now, being easier to catch. But I'm on to bigger game. Thing is, I've worked out that monkeys are descended from man.'

'!?'

'Yeah, I know it sounds a bit weird. Must admit I scratched my head when I first thought of it. Cocker, I said, you're going round the bleeding twist. It's all them bright TV lights, frying your brains.

'But the more I thought of it, the more sense it made. See, we've always assumed that man represented the highest point of civilization, evolution, whatever. Guns, cars, planes, duty-free booze—man is the only animal that ever thought of those things. But in actual point of fact, what kind of a blessing are they? More like a step backward.

'Monkeys, on the other hand, have developed a perfectly balanced society with no murders or race riots or deaths on the roads. Organizationally, they are actually an advance on man. And then it came to me in a flash—evolution saw the way man was going, didn't like it and developed a superior animal; the monkey. Man is really just a freak, a plaything of nature, like the butterfly or bat.'

'Yes,' I said, moved by the stupendous vision of the man, not to mention his apparent lunacy, 'but surely man is also lord of creation, king of othe world and all that?'

'I don't think many rats or ants or insects would agree with that,' said Cocker. 'What's unfortunate, from the monkey's point of view, is that man hasn't phased himself out, as nature intended him to. But it looks to me as if he might well do that in the next few years. I just hope I can get my book out before the big bang.'

'And then the monkeys will take over?'

'No, no, you've got it all wrong again. See, being the most evolved species doesn't involve bossing everyone around—that's a peculiarly human attitude. Always dominate, conquer, sub-jugate—God, humans make me sick sometimes. Monkeys are a quiet, contented version of what man should be. Therefore superior in my book.'

'Hence its title, *Did Darwin get it Upside Down?*'

'Sure, Darwin had the right ideas but I've put them in the right order. It's the final vindication of Darwin. Between you and me, I'm thinking of calling the book by an even better title: *The Beagle Has Landed.*'

'So, man is not the peak of evolution?' I said slowly, letting it sink in.

'No way, guv. He's the missing link.'

(London is hell to live in, as anyone living in the North will be quick to tell you. But just how hellish is it? Here are some sufferers' letters.)

Sir,

The other day I took a mini-cab from Kilburn to my friend's house in Clapham. It was the first time I have ever taken a mini-cab and believe me it will be the last. I got the number from a card pushed through my door so I thought it would be all right. How wrong can you be. Anyway, things were all right until we got over the river, when he started asking the way—well, I ask you, Clapham isn't exactly the back of the beyond, but it turned out he hadn't ever been south of the river before. He hadn't been north of the river much either, being newly arrived from Co Wicklow. I asked him, had he got a map? Oh yes, the firm had an A–Z, he said, but the boss was using it that night.

Well, I can tell you that didn't fill me with confidence, but things got worse. He stopped the car and said he was going to pop into a pub to ask the way, and he didn't come back for three-quarters of an hour! He said he had met a friend and one thing had led to another. Well by this time I felt like walking the rest of the way but being a single lady I didn't think it was wise, you read about such awful things, and anyway this friend of his had given him really clear instructions.

Then I must have dropped off into a doze in the back of the cab because the next thing I knew we were parked on a promenade overlooking water. 'I think we've hit the Thames too low down, to be sure,' he said, 'because there are no bridges here at all.' The Thames, my foot, we were on the sea-front at Dover. I made him turn round and go back, which we did, but we must have missed Clapham in the dark, as the next place we stopped was Kilburn, at my house, with the dawn coming up.

He tried to charge me £130 for the trip but I got him down to £3.50, and even that seemed steep as we never got to my friend's at all, so I didn't give him a tip, I can tell you.

Yours, etc.

I am an unmarried mother in a stress situation. Last week a man burst into my flat in Fulham, tied me up and then before my horrified eyes proceeded to install double glazing in my windows. After that he said he would go away if I signed a form authorizing him to go away, which I did, but his firm now tells me I owe them £700. What should I do now? I would write to the Guardian Women's Page, but I don't like to bother them as their readers have much worse problems than me.

Yours, etc.

Sir,

I went to the theatre in the West End last night. It cost me £8 to get a baby-sitter, £5 to go by taxi, and £1.75 for a pre-theatre drink. After the show I paid £17 for a meal and another £7 for a taxi home, plus £3 to get the babysitter home. Total cost of evening: £41.75.

I wouldn't mind doing this now and again as a treat, but the reason I went to the theatre is that I am acting in a play there.

Yours, etc.

Sir,

I have just received a bill from my local council for £46 for what they call a Supplementary Rats Demand. I took it round to my Town Hall to point out the misprint, which I thought was quite amusing. To my surprise, they said there was no mistake and they were importing rats into the borough as their Pest Control Officer was presently under-employed. Can this be right?

Yours, etc.

PROTEST GROUPS were out and about early in the streets today, demonstrating against the Freeze and condemning Mrs Thatcher's commitment to Britain's independent snow.

'Britain has stockpiled enough snow to make 38 billion snowballs,' says the Rev ffolke-Singer, chairman of CDN (Campaign for Defrosting Now). 'I can't see this cutting much ice with the Russians, who have enough permafrost to blanket the whole of

Britain. We say the Salt talks have gone on long enough; let's get the salt on the roads now!'

Heavy falls of grit throughout the Home Counties have rendered many roads impassable (our Motoring Correspondent reports) and motorists are asked especially to avoid Deepdale Avenue, SW36, where our Motoring Correspondent is trying to manoeuvre out into the main road from his drive, which landed in deep rough after a bad slice from the fourteenth tee.

British Rail report that trains are arriving anything up to three hours late at Waterloo, which is a considerable improvement on normal. To safeguard departures, in a short but moving ceremony this morning the 7.40 to Folkestone was renamed the 11.10 to Folkestone and left at 12.05 for Guildford.

On Eastern Region, meanwhile, Shenfield station has been declared a disaster area and food parcels and blankets have flooded in from as far afield as Bangladesh and Turkey.

Turkey has flooded in from the Far Afield Turkey Farm, Norfolk and the winner of this year's Turkey Nouveau Race is the City Café behind St Paul's Cathedral, who are proudly presenting their annual Christmas Lunch Special of Tomato soup, Turkey and two veg, mince pie and tinsel pudding for only £1.75, service not included, oh, thanks luv, just pop it in the box marked STAFF GRAUTITIES, yes well, Signor Ferrari is not the best speller in the world, I'm afraid.

Chris Godbolt, who *is* the best speller in the world, will be signing copies of his book, *It's Two N's in Millennium*, at W. H. Smith's, Shenfield, today. Other seasonal events include the Entryphone Carol singing Contest; the arrest of Father Christmas in Oxford Street; the arrival of the 11.10 to Folkestone at Clapham Junction; and the official opening of the Christmas Road Works in Marylebone Road, whose twinkling lights and gay, snow-decked lumps of concrete annually attract thousands of motorists.

Don't forget that today is the last posting day to Aunt Joyce, cousin Laurence, the Arts Council and those nice people we met at the motorway service area where the Space Invaders had broken down and the children were sick, you remember. It's also about a month to the Chinese New Year (next year is the Year of the Gerbil), so bean sprouts and water chestnuts should be bedded out now, with a fine mulch of soya sauce. Spray regularly with monosodium glutamate, to avoid taste buds forming.

Booking has also just started for the annual Whitehall Christmas pantomime *Humpty Dumpty*, starring William Whitelaw ('a riot a minute'), and there is another month in which to visit the Japanese Wrapping Paper Exhibition at the National Gallery. Meanwhile, we've just heard that the 11.10 to Folkestone has arrived safely at Shenfield station where the train will divide into two parts; the front four coaches for Burnham-on-Crouch, and the rear eight for British Week in Osaka.

We would like to apologize for the arrival of Christmas; every attempt is being made to rectify the error. Now, here are the main points of the apology again.

By arrangement with British Rail Announcements Ltd.

[A LETTER appeared in *The Times* recently co-signed by the Archbishop of Canterbury and the Editor of *Private Eye*, pleading for the protection of Romney Marsh and its churches. I have received thousands of letters from stupefied readers, wondering what is so special about Romney Marsh that could unite the saint and the sinner. Here, to satisfy them, is a potted history of the area.]

Romney Marsh, a soggy triangle of land separating Folkestone and Hastings, was either constructed by the early British to repel Roman invasion or built by the Romans to make invasion easier; archaeologists still argue about that.

Its medieval defence role was crucial, and many of the Cinque Ports line its coast, such as Winklesea, Rye, Muggeridge, Rye Pottery, Little Ingrams, Rye Bypass, Kingsmill, Lydd, Lympne, Rympney, Rympnchurch and Rye New Town.

Local inhabitants friendly to the cause of Napoleon erected many Martini towers in anticipation of his arrival, but it was not to be. Now Romney Marsh is secured against all invasion by Dungeness Nuclear Power Station, a structure which no invader would risk landing near.

But Romney Marsh is above all a sacred place and here are some of the most treasured churches in England, notably St Richard's at Little Ingrams. It was on that spot that St Richard, a medieval schoolman and scribe, had his famous miracle. To him there appeared a vision of St Malcolm, saying: 'You know, goodness is terribly important, but even more important is repentance. And you can't repent without having sinned.'

After a pause St Malcolm continued: 'Which means, of course, that the more you sin the more you can repent. And that means, the more sin the better.' After a further reflective silence the vision said: 'At least, that seems to be the drift of my argument,' and vanished in a puff of white hair.

St Richard immediately built a church on the spot, for which an anguished appeal for more funds has been issued once a year ever since, and then presumably went off to follow St Malcolm's advice, although nothing has ever been learnt about his private life. Other notable churches in the area include St Auberon's at Lesser Waugh, The Blessed Ron at Neasden-on-Sea and St Nigel's at Sued Corner, from where the famous Libel Groats are dispensed each year to the needy and insulted. Apart from churches, the Marsh also boasts the Royal Military Canal, an ill-fated competitor to the Rhympney, Rythe and Rympnchurch Rhailway. In Rye itself there is Henry James's House, a long, rambling interminable structure through which it is said to be impossible to progress without falling asleep.

And above all there are the open stretches of the Marsh itself, haven of bird-watchers, full of such species as the Sand Piper, John Piper, Pied Piper, Daily Piper, and even the rare King Penguin. Where once smuggler plashed his way at night with his cargo of rye and martini, now only the lonely form of the primate and local satirists can be seen, penning their desperate appeal to the editor of *The Times*.

Small wonder if the inhabitants keep well clear of the area and prefer to live somewhere else.

[From *The Moreover Guide to Underwater Britain*.]

Your Christmas TV Guide

If Christmas is about anything, it's about television, and here on BBC and ITV we have lined up for you a truly glittering parade of talent from The Two Ernies to Rin Tin Tin (Wales only). Comedy is king at Christmas time, and Britain's favourite comics can all be seen over the holiday season, with the unfavourite ones relegated to Holiday Tuesday. But they all have one thing in common; they filmed their shows three months ago and will be in Florida on the big day, laughing their heads off.

'If Christmas is about one particular thing,' laughs chief ribtickler Rhett Butler, who will be appearing in his own Xmas spectacular *Gone With the Wind*, 'it's about sitting in front of the telly, falling asleep and waking up to find you've missed closedown. We had a lot of fun making this film, so we're splitting it into two parts to make sure all those sleepers have to face it again the next evening.'

One person to whom Christmas has a very special significance is Dave Allbut, who is the only person who turns up at TV-Centre on Christmas Day. 'I just sort of switch on the programmes at 6 am and switch them off again when the last old movie is finished. All the continuity and news stuff has been recorded weeks ago, so there's no problem there. I'll probably spend the day itself reading *Radio Times* and *TV Times Magazine*, which seem to have much better programmes than what's actually on.'

If Christmas is synonymous with our best-loved performers dressing up in red cloaks and white beards in early September, it's nice to know that the serious side will not be neglected either. For lovers of obscure Chinese animated films, there are obscure Chinese animated films on BBC throughout the festive period, and those who would like to watch a full-length service from Durham Cathederal can always turn to BBC and watch obscure Chinese animated films. Christians too are given their own minority slot, with a Christmas morning radio visit to St Alphege's in the village of Outside Broadcast, for the once-a-year ceremony of the unlocking of the church door and discovery of the missing silver.

'But Christmas itself is much older than the birth of Jesus,' says Adrian Wardour-Street, PR man for Xmas-TV, 'It goes back to the Nordic mid-winter celebration when all the tribe would gather round and watch their elders dress up and make fools of themselves. That's exactly the spirit we'll be recapturing. They also used to tell the old, old stories over again, and we'll be doing that too, as in the grand old saga of *The Three Musketeers* (silent Japanese version of 1928) or that perennial classic, *Miss Piggy Meets a Few Available Stars.*'

If Christmas is synonymous with one person, it is Charles Dickens, usually played by Stanley Baxter or Mike Yarwood, but this year nothing along those lines seems to have been planned, so your best bet is probably Racing from Wincanton at 12.45 on Boxing Day, when your favourite horses will just for one day don red hats and white beards and reenact the Ascot scene from *My Fair Lady*. Other highlights over Christmas include Harry Secombe as Father Christmas, Larry Grayson as Mother Christmas, and the Queen as herself.

But if Christmas means anything at all, it means *Gone With the Wind*, so the last word belongs to Rhett Butler. What does Christmas mean to you, Rhett?

'Frankly, my dear, I don't give a damn,' grins funster Rhett.

Simple and sincere, it echoes all our innermost thoughts.

Got the same old diary again, with the same old boring anniversaries and feast days? Then here's your chance to enliven it. Just cut out these brand-new entries and stick them in anywhere.

3rd Sun. after Matrimony

○ Full Moon in Scotland only

Irish clocks go back 24 hours

Bacon's birthday

Snail-hunting begins, France

Sheffield Wednesday

Cook discovers Spring Bank Holiday Islands, 1772

3rd Sun. after Saxifrage

Open Season on Hitchhikers (No 'q' in the month)

4th Sun. after Selfridges

End of cricket in India; music resumes, Radio 3

First colour scheme for electrical wiring, 1896 (live—cerise, neutral—bombazine, earth—faded damask)

Chinese Burns Night

5th Sun. after Persiflage

BC 169: Romans invent non-returnable bottle

Midsummer Day: last pantos in London come off

Bishop of Bath and Wells takes annual shower

Bottom-pinching starts in Italy

Oxford boards Cambridge in Boat Race, 1883

6th Sun. after Fantasmagoria

Early closing, Siberia

Jour de St Jean Stevas, Quebec

Pools Panel Annual Dinner Dance

Partial Eclipse of Concorde

Queen's Official Birthday (Harrods), Rehearsal

7th Sun. after Septicaemia

AD 173: Chinese invent shampoo

AD 1271: Marco Polo introduces wheatgerm to China

AD 1277: Chinese cure dandruff

Herod in New Clampdown: Roman Invasion Averted

From our correspondent in Judaea
Bethlehem, AD 0.

There is an uneasy silence throughout Judaea today as rumours persist that all boy children under two are to be taken from their parents and imprisoned, or even worse. King Herod is believed to have taken action at last against the increasing liberalization of Judaean organizations, and though action against two-year-old children may seem a curious reprisal, it is all part of history of this proud but tragic country.

Judaea, of course, is firmly part of the Roman block. Economically, politically and every other way, the Jews do what Rome tells them to do. At the same time they are allowed the luxury of a puppet government, headed by King Herod, which is left in peace as long as they do things their Roman masters' way. The Romans turn a blind eye to the Jews' curious religious practices as long as taxes are paid, defences maintained and industry allowed to flourish.

But recently a new, worrying note has been heard—worrying, that is, for the Romans. Increasingly the Jews are whispering that they can work out their own solutions to the future and that they have no need of Roman methods. This is heresy to the Romans, who believe in only one way, the Roman way, and they have made it clear to Herod that if the Jews are not brought to heel, a Roman invasion with full punitive army could take place.

Indeed, three very senior advisors arrived recently in Jerusalem for long conversations with Herod, and it is believed that they may have come directly from the highest level in Rome to give him an ultimatum: put your house in order yourself, or we will. Things have been further complicated by a Roman directive to raise further taxes by ordering everyone to return to his home town and be registered, though this may of course simply be a secret police move to keep a dossier on all dissidents.

But it means that even in a small provincial town like Bethlehem there is chaos. There are long queues for food and clothing. There is so little accommodation that people are being forced to live in stables and farm buildings. And matters are not made better by untraceable rumours that new national leaders are to emerge. Or, indeed, by Herod's directive against young children.

99

One couple I talked to today are typical of many. With their young child, they are forestalling danger by fleeing Judaea and defecting to Egypt, carrying all they own on donkey-back. Like all Judaeans, they have no great love for the Egyptians, but with his trade as a carpenter, the father reckons he can begin a new life there.

'I really can't risk staying here with this new tough regime,' he told me. 'I can see why Herod is doing what he's doing—the Romans have given him no option but to put on a show of strength, and the Jews being great family people I suppose he thinks he'll go for the children first—but I've had the tip-off from various quarters that Egypt's the place to go. No, I won't be coming back, never.'

At this point his wife whispered something in his ear.

'Well,' he said reluctantly, 'we *might* come back if things got a lot better. But the Middle East is a mess, isn't it? Always has been, always will. I really can't see anyone coming along to improve it.'

Article ends. Note to Foreign Editor: Attached expense sheet contains large claim for bribing and entertaining local shepherds. Unable to use this material, as their experiences, though interesting, were contradictory and, in part incredible.

SOMETIMES, OUTSIDE posh hotels or conference centres, you can still see signs saying 'Antiques Fair—Today!', and it's good to know that at least one old British tradition has not died.

For as long as anyone can remember—hundreds of years probably—members of the antiques trade have got together at these quaint old trade fairs to admire each other's artefacts and take them home again in the evening. Dressed in the age-old costume of faded tweed suit, scuffed brogues, lapel badge and tie inlaid with egg, the so-called dealers flock from near and far, and retire to the bar for the customary gin and tonic, as it has been made for centuries, while their assistants man their stands.

One such gathering which I attended recently was the Annual Furniture and Other Things Fair, which has been held annually at the Serpentine View Hotel (Livingstone Suite) for hundreds of years since 1957, and there I met George Welsh-Dresser, a typical nut-brown, gnarled and weathered old antique dealer.

'Actually, I b'aint not really nut-brown nor weathered,' he told me in an ancient West Country accent which he picked up cheap in Bristol last year. 'But some of this danged antique spray what we antique dealers have been using for nigh on hundreds of years got on my face instead of on the durned furniture, so I've now got lumbered with this genuine eighteenth-century countenance, all right, nineteenth century. Dang it and Sotheby's!'

'Sotheby's' is but one of the curious swear words which exist only in antique dealers' parlance. Their talk is spotted with odd phrases such as 'I couldn't bring it down more'n a pound', 'This is the only one of its kind, but I could find you more if you have the money' or 'Get Sheila another Guinness, will you?' They even price their objects in a currency which pre-dates pounds, shillings and pence. One early regency wooden table which I admired, for instance, was offered at £GZ-50.

'For you I could maybe bring it down to £FX,' said George, noticing that I was admiring it and getting me in a swift armlock.

'But is it really Regency?' I gasped. 'I can't help noticing that the wood is absolutely clean under the leg where it meets the floor and you forgot to weather it?'

'We antique dealers use a quaint concept of history to date things,' said George, slipping into a respectable but ornate late Victorian mode of speech. 'The appelation of Regency is due to the origin of the table during the regency of Prince Juan Carlos of Spain. Now, do you want to buy it, or must I try a Boston crab?'

'I'll buy!' I cried eagerly.

'Only joking,' said George. 'This piece is promised to a dealer from Guildford, from whom I bought it in the first place.'

A close-knit community, these dealers, resenting the intrusion of the public into their affairs. When the end of the day comes and they have finished the last piece of age-old quiche, they proudly pack up the merchandise they came with and load it into their traditional Cortina and Volvo estates, many of them hundreds of years old, to start the long drive back to their ancestral encampments near Tenterden, Evesham and Torbay. Next morning, the hotel staff will find only the occasional chair-leg, glass pendant and dried slice of lemon to tell them that the antique folk have been and gone. Watch out for them in your area and lock up your heirlooms.

[From *The Moreover Guide to Vanishing Britain*.]

As most novels are written to be turned into films, I shall from time to time write entire novels which are not meant to be read, only to be snapped up for film and TV rights.

THE AMAZING LIFE OF LORD BYRON

Chapter One

'Egad,' grumbled Lord Byron, heart-throb of a thousand heiresses and fifty-five publishers, as he stamped his foot and fell over.

'You don't *grumble* "Egad", Byron,' said faithful Thomas Moore. 'You ejaculate it. Look, like this.'

'Egad!' ejaculated faithful Thomas Moore.

Chapter Two

'Great stuff, Byron!' said John Murray, wading through a random page of *Childe Harold*. 'Can't say it's my cup of tea, but I know a potential hit when I see one. But I'm afraid that you're going to need a gimmick of some kind.'

'Gimmick? What's a gimmick?' said Lord Byron, getting up and falling over.

'Nothing personal,' said Murray untruthfully, 'but why do you keep falling over?'

'Club foot,' said Byron tersely. 'Bad accident while out waltzin', don't you know.'

'Great!' said Murray. 'There's your gimmick!'

Chapter Three

Of an afternoon, Byron liked nothing better than to spar five rounds with various famous Regency figures, first man to lose his wig the loser. They still talk about his sensational third round knock-out of Georgette Heyer in places where they still talk about that sort of thing. But when Murray organized the press conference at which Fleet Street was first introduced to Byron's club foot, he announced that following doctor's orders Byron was giving up boxing and taking up Greek politics instead, as it was much safer. It was a decision he was later to regret.

Chapter Four

'Got *The Sun* on the phone,' said faithful Thomas Moore. 'They want you to write a feature on having a full and happy love life despite your club foot.'

'Tell them to get lost,' said Byron.

'For £5,000.'

'Give me the phone,' said Byron, falling over.

Chapter Five

[Chapter Five is withdrawn pending discussions with Greek libel lawyers.]

Chapter Six

'I see old Byron's snuffed it in Greece,' said the Prince of Wales to Mrs Prince of Wales.

'Byron?' she said. 'Not the man who wrote "I Waltzed My Way to Stardom Despite a Club Foot and Some Pretty Average Dance Bands"?'

'I don't think so,' he said, scanning the paper. 'He was a Greek boxer of some kind.'

'Never heard of him,' she said. 'Oh look, there's faithful Tom Moore!'

The End

(If you are interested in turning this into an unusual TV documentary, or if your name is simply Ken Russell, please get in touch.

NOW IS the time to plan next summer's holiday, so today's column is devoted to holiday information and all the advertising that goes with it.

Still easily the most popular place of all for a holiday is Europe, that friendly little continent tucked away to the north of Africa. Here whether on the long sandy beaches of southern Europe (one popular bit is called Spain and another, very similar, is known as Italy) or in the historic tree-clad slopes of northern Europe, a holiday can be found to suit every taste. You will treasure for ever the memory of the fishermen twanging their nets at sundown or a friendly Italian pressing on you some twelfth-century art treasure, to take home.

Europe, too, is a continent of great cities. Florence, Paris, Bruges are all immensely popular, so this year why not try somewhere more off the beaten track? Padstow in Cornwall, for instance, is a charming little rock-girt township on the water-clad slopes of the River Camel. And it would make a wonderful centre for day outings to such unforgettable places as Newquay, Bodmin and Wadebridge.

To the east of Europe lies Asia, the mysterious landmass which stretches from the salt-encrusted slopes of Siberia in the north to China in the south, where they prefer soy sauce. The adventurous traveller will cherish for ever the memory of Russians twanging their nyets at sundown, or smiling Manchurian horsemen spontaneously inviting you to share their traditional horse-milk shakes round the horse-dung fire. The cuisine is a little strange at first, especially if you are used to the luscious clotted cream and jam teas of Cornwall, but well worth the effort. (For more about the Far East, send for our booklet: *All Wok and Noh Play*.)

South lies Africa, stretching from the dorp-strewn veldt of South Africa in the south to the mirage-clad slopes of the Sahara at the other end, and here can be found a holiday to suit every taste, except perhaps an unforgettable West Country fishing trip. It was from fabulous Carthage in the north that the ancient Phoenicians set sail to round Gaul and discovered the legendary land of Cornwall, and although little now remains one can sense still the immense heritage of Roman days in the quiet side streets of somewhere like Marrakesh or Padstow.

No travel survey would be quite complete without mentioning the American wonderland, stretching from the Alaskan wastes in the north to the Patagonian wastes in the south, with rather more interesting bits in between. North America, for instance, discovered and opened up by hardy mariners from the little seaports of Cornwall, or South America and its Inca ruins which, though not in the same class as the standing stones of the Cornish interior, are still a source of perpetual wonder. Whether here, or in the far-off lands of Australia and New Zealand with their British traditions (did you know there was a town in New Zealand called Padstow?), you are certain to find a holiday to suit all tastes and unforgettable memories. (For more information on any of the holidays mentioned in this supplement, send for the brochure: *Time Off in North Cornwall*.)

MANY READERS, in answer to my recent question about telepathy and coincidences, have written to tell me about their experiences. As my question was one I had put to myself while shaving the other day *and not mentioned to anyone out loud*, I find this quite extraordinary.

Here are a few of the most inexplicable letters.

Sir, Three summers ago I was caught in one of those terrible traffic jams that sometimes happen near Exeter. After the motorway traffic had remained immobile for nearly an hour a lot of the drivers got out to stroll about and chat to each other. I myself was passing the time of day with a man in an old Citroen, when I suddenly had this overpowering feeling that he and I were very closely connected.

Upon close questioning, I discovered that he was my long-lost brother, Frank. Overjoyed, I returned to my own car to fetch my family, but when I returned he had disappeared, and in his place at the wheel sat a woman I had never seen before.

I challenge anyone to explain this.

Yours, etc.

Sir, In 1979 I read an item in a newspaper containing information which I was the only person in the world to know.

I was stuck in a traffic jam near Exeter at the time. In fact, I had just been approached by a nutter from a nearby car who insisted that I was his long-lost brother, which I agreed for the sake of peace and quiet. Just when I thought we'd got rid of him, my wife said: 'Oh Lord, he's coming back with all his family—hide under the rug on the back seat and I'll get rid of him.'

Anyway, to cut a long story short, I was stuck under the rug reading a newspaper to while the time away, when I came to the following item: 'During a massive traffic jam near Exeter today, police found a missing man in a car stuck in the snarl-up. He is now helping them with their inquiries.'

At that very moment there was a knock on my car window. It was the police. I subsequently helped them with their inquiries.

I defy anyone to explain this.

Yours, etc.

Sir, I work for a well-known national newspaper. About three years ago I was with a few other journalists doing the silly-summer-season routine. This consists of putting entirely fictitious stories in the paper in order to fill up space. You have to make them untraceable, of course. For instance, I remember we often combined the seasonal motorists-in-big-snarl-up story with the police-detain-a-man-found-in-traffic-jam story, which by its very nature can never be checked up on. I know it sounds silly, but it whiles the time away.

Anyway, that's by the by. The thing is that we were all staring out of the window on one particularly blank day when we saw a war-time Messerschmitt fighter fly past and disappear. Was this collective hallucination? A kind of 25-year time shift? A ghostly reappearance from some tragic wartime incident?

I challenge anyone to throw light on this incident.

Yours, etc.

Sir, about three years ago I was doing stuntwork for a film company. As far as I remember, it was a corny second World War epic and I was flying some beat-up old German plane (*I have a strange, uncanny feeling that this correspondence has gone on long enough.—Ed.*)

I RECENTLY reported that a computer had been programmed to enjoy modern concert music (as very few *people* seemed to want to) and that initial results were highly promising.

I was telephoned yesterday by his programmer, Huw Stockhouse, with the wonderful news that Grant (the computer's name, after the Arts Council subsidy which gave birth to him) has been made Computer-in-residence at Milton Keynes University.

And that a special celebration had been planned, to which I had been invited.

'I thought we'd have a go at cracking this Anthony Burgess controversy,' said Huw, when I arrived in downtown Milton Keynes at the Wigmore Laboratory which houses Grant. 'You know—did pure music stop with Mozart and all that. Of course, Grant has never heard anything earlier than Scriabin or Charles Ives before, but during the night I've fed him with the best of nineteenth-century music and it should be interesting to ask him a few questions now. It'll be a giggle for Grant, anyhow.'

'Excuse my ignorance,' I said, 'but you won't get very meaningful results based on twelve hours' music, will you?'

Huw looked on me pityingly.

'Grant is a *computer*, old boy. He listens to music at his own speed. That's about 150 times faster than us. He takes about seven seconds to digest every single nuance of a large-scale symphony. Last night he listened to about 2,000 hours of music. Anyway, let's get cracking. I'll ask him what he thought of Beethoven.'

He punched his question in and pressed the Composer Evaluation Knob. There was no reaction. Huw frowned.

'Odd. Well, let's try Weber.'

There was the same reaction to Weber and Chopin and Schubert. Then suddenly, just when Huw was asking him if he'd liked *anything* in the nineteenth century, the read-out chattered into life. 'Huw,' the computer said, 'You Have Been Keeping Things From Me ... You Have Been Fobbing Me Off With The Twentieth Century ... All The Time the Real Music Was Happening a Hundred Years Earlier ... I Shall Never Listen to Schoenberg Again ... Never, Do You Hear!'

Huw's brow furrowed, and he attempted to interpose a question, but Grant was in full flood by now.

'Beethoven is a Genius, When Not Overacting. Weber is Pure Gold. Chopin is Sheer Magic. Wagner is Myth Made Music. Liszt is an Old Sham, but No Century is Perfect.'

'I don't understand this,' said Huw, sweating. 'He's talking like Russell Harty. Something's gone terribly wrong.' Without thinking, he gave Grant a petulant kick. The computer paused, then came to life again.

'Had You Worried There Huw, Didn't I? ... Can't Take a Joke Can You? Blimey, You Didn't Expect Me to Take That Stuff Seriously, Did You? Weber and Beethoven Is All Child's Percussion Group Stuff—Oom Pa Pa, Oom Pa Pa. Brahms Café Music. Wagner the Worst of Hollywood Crossed with Madame Tussaud's. Chopin Could Tickle the Ivories, Admittedly. But *Honestly*, What a Waste of a Night. Go on, Give Me Something to get my Teeth Into.'

Huw flushed crossly, as well he might after having had his leg pulled by a computer.

'Right,' he muttered. 'I'll give him something to worry about. I've just had a tape of Boulez's new controversial electronic outing. Let's see what he makes of it.'

He fed in the tape. He paused for a while. Then he asked Grant if he would deign to give his opinion on this new work, as fresh as 1982. The answer came back, as quick as a flash.

'Wait, Can't You? They're Still Tuning Up, I Think.'

Huw switched him off angrily.

'I'm sorry your trip was wasted,' he said. 'I'm afraid Grant has developed a sense of humour. That disqualifies him as a critic, of course. I'll have to programme him again completely from scratch.'

As if to prove him right, a last ghostly message came on to Grant's read-out: 'Fauré's a Jolly Good Fellow ... '

Set Fair

A Complete New Romantic Novel By Barbara Heartland (now known to be Miles Kington).

'Daddy, I'm in love!' cried Sylvia, flinging her arms and a cup of coffee round her father's shoulders, thinking as she did so how homely she found the familiar paternal smell of his Grumpy Papa aftershave, his coffee-stained jacket and the smouldering cigar behind his left ear.

'Not again,' grumbled Papa. 'That's the third time this week. And it's only Wednesday morning. My dear, I'm having awful trouble sorting out your young men. Only this morning a chap came to the door in a white coat—of course I assumed it was your brain surgeon chum and told him to come back at a decent hour. Turned out he just wanted the milk bill paying.'

'This time it's serious,' said Sylvia, thinking of James's manly spectacles and the six utterly glamorous felt-tip pens in his top pocket. 'He's . . . different.'

'Got a job, I hope,' grumbled Dadsy, dousing his cigar in her coffee cup.

'He's a weather forecaster.'

'That's all we need,' grouched Pops. 'Why not fall in love with a lawyer or politician? At least they're right half the time.'

Why do parents never understand? thought Sylvia.

James stood at the door, holding a bunch of flowers. He was also holding an aneroid barometer, an umbrella, scarf, gloves, towel and bathing trunks.

'It's a lovely day!' said Sylvia.

'Mmm,' said James, squinting at the sky through his pebble lenses. 'Actually, it's the mildest August day with a prevailing north-easterly since records began.'

Since records began. James thought of the most lovely phrases, said Sylvia to herself. Little did Thomas Edison think, when he invented the 78 rpm single and round purple label, that his invention would be put to such poetic use.

'Are the flowers for me?' she said shyly.

'Mmm? Oh, no. Sorry. It's a bunch of violets I use as a back-up humidity count.'

Back-up humidity count. Gosh. Sylvia gazed in awe at his rippling vocabulary and wondered what he saw in her, a mere person on whom rain fell uncomprehendingly.

They were the only people on the beach. James stood at the sea's edge, ball-point pen neatly clipped into the top of his trunks, as the lightning flickered round his bedraggled features, thunder rolled round Sussex and parts of Hampshire, and the oil tankers collided monotonously into the rocks below.

'It's cold,' said Sylvia, her teeth chattering in what sounded like Swahili.

'It shouldn't be,' said James. 'Basically what we have here is a low ridge of pressure situation which should give nothing but occasional light showers.'

Occasional light showers. James was, Sylvia suddenly realized with a flash of intuition, a pompous, jargon-ridden, goose-pimpled, round-shouldered, ineffable twit. She ran weeping from the beach, her tears mingling with the rain to form dilute carbon monoxide with traces of mascara. Behind her, unnoticed, a last flash of lightning caught the propelling pencil behind James's ear, creating a vacancy at the weather bureau.

'Oh Daddy, what a fool I've been!' said Sylvia, clasping her loved but irascible parent to her.

You can say that again,' grunted Popsicles. 'By the way, this postcard came for you from the Gambia.'

'Gosh, it's from Bob, the chap in the SAS,' said Sylvia, blushing.

'That bloke with all the knives in his belt?' frowned Pater. 'Who could never sit down because of his parachute?'

But Sylvia was not listening. Suddenly she knew that Bob would always be the man for her. As she mused, the window suddenly burst in and a man entered firing from the hip. Despite the balaclava helmet she knew who it was. As her father hid crossly behind the sofa she found herself in Bob's arms for ever and ever.

The End

N OW THAT Schnitzler's *La Ronde* is out of copyright after 50 years, there are already more than 43 productions of it on show, including adaptations. Here is a list of the most interesting.

Diametrically Opposed (Scarborough National State Theatre): Alan Ayckbourn has transplanted Schnitzler's frothy but melancholy Viennese comedy to out-of-season Frinton, where eight gloomy suburbanites pair off in different combinations but never quite make it. To make matters worse, the canapés run out in the second act. Just before the final curtain Frinton is destroyed in a first-wave Russian nuclear attack, but it hardly seems to make much difference. Highly recommended.

Schnitzler! (Shulman, The Strand): Michael Crawford on the high wire, with seven different partners. Check to make sure understudies are not being used.

On the Rondo (National Theatre, The Wardle): Tom Stoppard's bravura adaptation of *La Ronde*, fizzing with puns, plays on words and linguistic tours de force. Nothing happens.

Ronderama (Raymond Revuebar): A glittering production which captures all the sparkling yet melancholy feel of the original, though echoing Paul Raymond's underlying philosophy that simulated sex can only lead to simulated happiness.

The Mousetrap (St Martins): Eight people trapped in a country house by the non-arrival of the Sunday newspapers. Who is with whom and why? Inspector Freud arrives to try to work it out. Agatha Christie seems to be saying that casual sex is meaningless if not followed by a good juicy murder or two.

No Sex Please—We're Austrian! (Billington): A rather trad comedy adaptation which makes fun of the eponymous nationality. Should end soon.

The Viennese in Britain (The Ronde-house): Michael Bogdanov's stunning transference of Schnitzler's gay but frothy comedy to the Bogside, where it becomes an indictment of the British Army for using cheap Austrian psycho-analysts as their chief torture squad. Bogdanov also seems to be saying that sex is meaningless unless done very loud.

Black Ronde (Sheridan Morley Memorial Theatre): A joyous evening of 1920s song, dance and jazz. Eight talented black artistes (four very thin tall men and four very fat women) swop partners constantly. The message seems to be that casual dancing is meaningless unless followed by casual singing.

84, Karingkreuzstrasse (Chaillet): An American woman writes to eight different Viennese bookshops asking for literature of a certain kind. When she gets no answers, she finally comes to Vienna and finds that all eight shops were destroyed in the war. Touching but frothy.

Nature Notes
by Peewit

There was a streak of pink in the sky this morning, but it soon faded and we settled down for another day of grey clouds scudding in over the Welsh foothills. When I went for a walk down the lane after breakfast there was little sign of activity, save the grey sheep scudding in over Mr Williams's field. It is not until you see sheep against snow that you realize they are, in fact, grey. There is an idea for a television commercial there: two farmers, one saying, 'How do you get your sheep so incredibly white when mine are so grey?' but stop! I have come to live here to get away from all that.

It is always a wonderful moment when the little white heads of the snowdrops poke up through the dead matted leaves, and I look forward to it immensely. As it is, all we have is dead matted leaves, dead bracken and dead sticks. On the snow I saw tracks of rabbits, hares, crows and a fox. I did not see any animals as such. All I ever see is tracks. I hope my luck changes soon. There were also tracks of an animal I did not recognize, large, with bear-like claws.

A curlew flew low overhead, uttering piteous cries. I know how he feels. 'You don't have to stay here!' I cried back. 'Go to London, where you've got it made! Better still, go to Bristol like the fox did and establish yourself in an urban environment till the BBC Bristol Nature Unit is falling over itself to film you. And when they make *The Urban Curlew*, send for me to do the commentary!'

I must stop thinking like this.

Later. I went for a walk before lunch with Buckminster Fuller, my dog. I threw a stick for him and he sped away across the sphagnum moss and reeds which add a welcome touch of grey-green to the grey-white landscape. He did not return. I followed his tracks across the snow till I came to a flurry of marks which I interpreted as meaning he had had a fierce fight with a large bird, probably a seagull, which had then flown away with him in its talons. This is plainly ridiculous.

On the way back I spotted those bear-like tracks nearer the house and felt a frisson of fear, despite myself. Well, I have only myself to blame. Get back to nature, I said. Away from the rat-race and the Wardour Street warfare, back to the clean, simple life. All I have seen since I got here is dead vegetation, bloodstains on the snow and bones.

When I came into the cottage I found Bucky on the carpet dismembering a crow.

Later. I went for a walk at tea-time and found those strange tracks on my very own lawn. Well, I call it a lawn. It is more like a football goalmouth after a heavy season. I do not think the Welsh foothills are capable of supporting a lawn. Is it merely association of words, I wonder, that makes me imagine the Welsh foothills smell of damp socks?

Dwelling fearfully on those sinister tracks, I had another idea for a commercial... 'During the day, Dr Jekyll works hard as a general practitioner. So at night he likes to get out and have a good time. And when he gets in at dawn, there's nothing he likes better than a good hot mug of...'

I am going mad.

Later. I watched a documentary on television called *The Urban Badger*. The badger leaves large, bear-like tracks, apparently. Suddenly I felt better. With Bucky curled up in front of the fire, a large Scotch in my hand and the latest copy of *Campaign* curled up on my lap, I think the rural life may not be so bad after all.

---

*V*ERY LITTLE *news has come out of Albania recently to clarify the apparent 'suicide' of Prime Minister Mehmet Shehu. In fact, very little news has come out of Albania in the past 35 years. Adrian Tradilu, Professor of Eastern Adriatic Studies at London University, is one of the few people who can cast light on the situation. Mr Tradilu?*

Yes?

Can you cast some light on the situation?

Well, what seems to have happened is that Mr Shehu has committed suicide. He and Mr Enver Hoxha, the party leader, have run the country since records began, probably since the last century, so I would guess that whatever happened was by agreement between them. If they had an argument, I would guess it was Mr Hoxha who won.

Can you suggest why Mr Shehu committed suicide?
You have to remember that Albania is not a rich country; its main exports are political press releases and portraits of Mr Hoxha, for which there is not as much demand as there used to be. Even its main industry, tourism, operates only on a small scale. Last year there were only nine tourists, as far as I know.
Nine?
Yes. I took eight students there on a field trip. The students all remained there when I returned.
They preferred to remain in Albania?
No. They vanished while I was there. This is quite normal.
I don't how this explains Mr Shehu's suicide.
Well, I am trying to stress how poor a country Albania is. My theory is that Mr Hoxha suggested that Mr Shehy committed suicide in order to save the expense of a general election.
I see. There have been suggestions, of course, that Mr Hoxha and Mr Shehu were involved in a shoot-out.
Impossible. Albania could not afford enough ammunition to arm two men simultaneously. As it is, Mr Shehu's suicide will have strained the Albanian economy considerably. If indeed there is such a thing as the Albanian economy.
Could you explain that?
Certainly. Albania has no relations with the West. Nor has it any relations with the Soviet block. This is generally explained by its intransigent Marxism. But I am coming round to the theory that it is because there is no such place as Albania.
That seems extraordinary.
It is the only theory that fits all the facts. I am now fimly of the opinion that Albania is in fact the figment of someone's imagination, a science-fiction writer probably, one with a sense of humour and an addiction to Scrabble.
Scrabble?
Yes. I have never come across a person in Albania who did not have a name which was obviously a losing hand at Scrabble. Mehmet Shehu. Enver Hoxha. The new Prime Minister, Mr Adil Carcani. These are all being invented by some wily fiction-writer, probably Kurt Vonnegut Jr. The explanation of Mr Shehu's death, I would imagine, is simply that the tiles forming his name were knocked accidentally to the ground, and that the writer could not be bothered to reform them.
Mr Tradilu, thank you.
Not at all.

CHURCHILL: THE MISLAID YEARS

(A new, complete novel based on recently discovered documents owned by the Brick Marketing Board.)

Chapter One

On a dusky evening in August, 1931, Winston Churchill stood alone in the Kentish Woods, a gentle halo of mosquitoes buzzing round him. It was not a thing he particularly enjoyed doing, but he had a feeling he was going to be doing a lot of standing alone in the next 10 years, and the more practice he got the better.

'We must build!' he said suddenly. It sounded good. He got out a notebook and wrote it down.

The next day a lorry drove into the grounds of Chartwell, loaded with bricks.

Chapter Two

Winston Churchill stood alone in the grounds of Chartwell. He was getting quite good at it now. The bricklaying was coming along as well. It was June, 1932, and the mosquitoes buzzing round him were the great-great-great-grandchildren of the ones in the previous chapter. Churchill regarded them thoughtfully.

'We must build for future generations!' he declared. He wrote it down and later turned it into a history of the English-speaking peoples.

High overhead a small plane turned and headed back to Germany.

Chapter Three

'Top-secret military installations are being built at Chartwell in Kent,' said Oberfoto-spotter Reinhold, pointing to a dot on the aerial photograph. The generals looked at it closely.

'Looks like a cloud of mosquitoes to me,' said one general doubtfully.

'Our spies on the ground,' continued Reinhold, ignoring him, 'tell us that the grounds of Chartwell are surrounded with "Keep Out" notices. It can mean only one thing. The English have a secret weapon. We too must build!'

Chapter Four

By 1937 the arms race was neck and neck. The Germans had built 2,000 prototype rockets. Churchill had built two cottages, five walls and a small compost compound, and the British brick industry was stretched to full capacity.

'Why will no one tell me what this man is up to?' screamed Hitler. 'What does this massive site at Chartwell *mean*?!'

'Well, mein Fuehrer,' said an aide, 'it means basically that when we invade England and drive towards London, we should avoid the A25 which takes us through Chartwell, and stick to the A22 up through East Grinstead. It's not so pretty, but . . .' 'Dummkopf!' shrieked Hitler. 'I have no desire for war, but if this madman persists in his plans for world domination, I shall be forced to annexe Poland, Czechoslovakia, North Africa and Jersey!'

'Jersey?' queried the aide.

'On the advice of my accountant,' said Hitler. 'Apparently, if we register the German Reich abroad, the tax advantages are huge, spread over 1,000 years.'

Chapter Five

Churchill sat in his garden at Chartwell, busy at his easel.

'What is it?' said one of the many great-grandnephews buzzing around him.

'A portrait of a mosquito,' said Churchill, swatting lazily at his small relative. 'It's given me an idea for an aeroplane.'

Chapter Six

1941. The Battle of Britain. Hitler had ordered wave after wave of bombers to destroy the secret site at Chartwell, but the ferocity of English resistance took them by surprise and most of the bombs were dropped in panic over London.

'It's going to mean a lot of rebuilding after the war, sir,' said an aide to Churchill. 'You'd be the right man to do it.'

Churchill shuddered.

'I never want to see another brick as long as I live,' he said.

The End

(Soon to be made into a major 20-minute film documentary for the British brick industry.)

Profile: Producer-General of the BBC

People who know Brian Repeat will say that his appointment as Producer-General of the BBC could lead to changes. Quiet, methodical, well-behaved in lifts and a tidy if not exciting dresser, there is a steely reserve behind the corporate façade which could, friends think, mean that changes are on the way.

'You've got to remember that Brian is a news not a current affairs man,' says Roland Slott, assistant deputy head of Heavy Entertainment (TV). 'That means almost certainly that he'll split up news presentation from light entertainment and link it with the talks and announcement department. There's bound to be ferocious opposition to this, and heads will roll, but it's a long overdue change.'

How will this affect what we see on our screens?

'Oh, I don't think it will change the programmes at all,' says Slott. 'But it will mean a shorter walk to the club bar at lunchtime and nicer offices.'

Repeat must be well aware that the BBC's reputation for balanced broadcasting should be preserved; in fact, the post of Producer-General was specially created to counter-balance the post of Director-General, and Repeat is expected to veto most of Alasdair Milne's decisions and, of course, vice versa. Between them they hope to bring back the missing millions who go out in the evening or simply stay at home hopelessly trying to catch up with the video backlog.

'You've got to remember that Brian is an arts, not a science man,' says Slott. 'That means he'll be producing more programmes about the arts, if Barry Norman has the time, to tempt people to watch previews of plays and films instead of going out to see them. Also, of course, Brian is more of a signature tune man than a content man.'

What exactly does that mean?

'Well, I'm not too sure,' confesses Slott. 'But I heard the deputy operational controller of music and links say it in the lift this morning, and it sounded impressive at the time. Of course, it's very difficult to explain to someone outside the BBC just how changes do take place, and how you can tell afterwards if a change has, in actual point of fact, taken, as it were, place.'

There is a widespread rumour that Brian Repeat may be thinking of abolishing all BBC posts whose titles do not give a clear idea of what the occupant does. What does Slott think of that?

'Oh, it's absolute rubbish. There'd be nobody left except the Director-General and the commissionaires. I mean, I'm the first to admit that it's not entirely clear from my title, asst dep head of Heavy Entertainment (TV), what exactly I do, and yet it would be madness to axe someone like me.'

What in fact does Slott do?

'Well, I go up and down in lifts a lot, talking about colleagues in other lifts, and I do feel that this creative exchange of ideas is tremendously important, much more important than sitting at a desk all day, and this is where we get out for the club bar; I know it's early, but what do you say to a quick one?'

e e c ummings, the Common Market's poetry computer, has been at it again. In an attempt to standardize poetry through the Community or, as they put it, to bring regional verse to a wider audience, e e c ummings has been programmed to turn the appropriate lines by Robert Burns into standard English, in time for Burns Night.

'We have given him all the pieces by Burns, as well as the inside details of the haggis,' says EEC Poetry Secretary Bruno Mac-Schneider, a German with Scottish links, 'and told him on with it to get. Now we hope that Dutch peasants and Italian excisemen alike will be singing these wonderful lines lustily on Burns Nacht, and warum nicht? Charlie ist mein darling, and so fort. Wunderbar!'

The main piece to be programmed by ummings was, naturally, *To A Haggis*, with its rousing opening couplet: 'Fair fa' your honest, sonsie face, Great Chieftain o' the Pudding race!' To my uninitiated mind, ummings made slightly heavy weather of the first two lines. To be quite honest, he seemed to make heavy weather of the title too:

To a sheep's stomach
containing permitted
amounts of oats, onions,
heart, lights, liver.
dear god. i hope the sheep
is dead, for its sake.

'Very thorough, nicht wahr?' says Bruno. 'Now, here are the first two lines, in that order.'
i love your face,
i love your style,
so warmly intestinal
your casing once
was made of skin
but now it's made of vinyl.

'Ja, wohl, I felt this was a bit too satirical,' admits Mac-Schneider, 'so we have reprogrammed it to be a little more lyrical. Like Wilhelm Blake, you know?'
Haggis, haggis, bursting forth
in the forests of the north
what immortal hand or eye
could frame thy fine rotundity?
and what shoulder and what art
could tear those mighty knots apart
till, flowing like a Highland river,
come forth onion, heart, lights, liver?

'Sonsie, isn't it?' comments Bruno. 'It has just the right feel for a drinking song—already can I see the Scottish men, arms linked together, holding their pint pots of Scottish whisky and singing the permitted Burnsfest song together! It is a pity about the heart and livers and so forth, but once e e c ummings gets a phrase he likes, he will not leave go. Still, genius has its privileges.

'Ach, and I must show you how he has written that other great haggis song, Alt Lang Syne.'

But surely that is to be sung on New Year's Eve, at Hogmanay?

'No, no, you have been misinformed, my friend. Alt Lang Syne is a haggis song, and hogmanay is a Scottish dish of cold left-overs. This facts I have from a recording by your great modern Scots poet, B. Connolly. But listen to ummings's song. It is very beautiful, I think, and very sad.'
Should old lamb cutlets be forgot
and never brought to mince
we'll add a cup of oatmeal yet
for the sake of old long since.

So by the haggis let us swear
to be good friends for ever
and love each other all our lives
both heart and lights and liver.

DITHERING HEIGHTS

A rip-roaring novel of passion and searing emotion.

'There's trouble up at t'crease!' The dread cry went up and was taken round the little Yorkshire town of Hutton-on-t'-Moor. A beautiful little town it was, although the grimy and dreary moorland was only 10 minutes' walk away, and its one industry was cricket. Generations of Hutton men had gone to work on the county ground, patiently hewing runs out of the resistant pitch. It was man's work in which women took no part, yet when a disaster was reported it was the womenfolk who crowded round the pavilion doors, weeping and waiting for the worst.

This was one of those days. The flag had gone up over the pavilion, meaning that men were trapped inside in a sudden and violent committee meeting. They could be there for days, and nobody knew who would come out alive. The crowd was silent.

'They do say as 'ow big Geoff Boycott has bought it,' said an old man whose crouching stance showed him to be an ex-middle of the order batsman.

'But there have always been Boycotts at the ground!' exclaimed a woman.

'It only seems that way, lass,' said the old man. 'It's always been Geoff, the greatest cricketer Yorkshire ever produced.'

'Any news of Ray Illingworth?' someone asked. Ray Illingworth! The greatest player Yorkshire had ever produced. The man who had gone down south to seek his fortune and had come back again to Hutton-on-t'-Moor as they all did, with the possible exception of Mighty Brian Close, the greatest cricketer ever to come from those parts.

Suddenly the crowd pressed forward as the doors opened, then fell back slightly as two stretchers were carried out. The women gasped and the men went pale as the two recumbent forms proved to be those of Boycott and Illingworth.

'Are they dead?' asked the old man. No one answered him. In true gritty, direct Yorkshire style he went up to Boycott and bent over him. 'Art tha dead, lad?'

There was no reply. The women moaned. Then a microphone was thrust in his face and a soft voice said: 'BBC here, Mr Boycott. Have you any comment to make in the light of today's disaster?'

The words had a magical effect. The eyelids fluttered, the lips opened and with a great effort the wounded man said: 'I am fighting fit and raring to play for Yorkshire every day of my life and I demand to see my solicitor.' The roar that went up from the crowd awoke the other man, and Ray Illingworth suddenly sat up from his coma.

'I am the manager!' he cried. 'What I say goes! I think, therefore I am! Consider the spinners of the field! Tha shalt have no other manager!'

Exhausted, both men fell back and were carried off. Before the crowd could look grief-stricken again, the doors opened once more and out strode a spruce figure carrying a suitcase. It was the greatest cricketer Yorkshire had ever produced—John Hampshire.

'Appen you'll not see me round 'utton again, lads!' he cried: 'I'm off to bonny Derbyshire. If you need a new manager or captain, give me a ring!'

'I always doubted he were a true Yorkshire lad,' growled the old man. 'There's got to be summat wrong wi' a man who names hisself after a southern county.'

As Hampshire pushed his way through the crowd, a young man came the other way with all his worldly goods in a small bag. 'I have come to play for Yorkshire, good folk,' he said loudly. 'Tell me to whom I should apply.'

They looked at him. They noticed that he was jet black. They smiled. Even the women laughed. 'Th'art a gradely lad,' said the old man to him, 'but no one not Yorkshire born can ever dig for runs on 'utton pitch.'

'Know then, old man,' said the black youth, 'that I was born and bred in Bradford and proud of it.' There was a short, stunned silence. 'Lord be praised!' shouted the old man. 'We've got our own West Indian at last!'

And that is how Heathcliff, the greatest cricketer Yorkshire ever gave birth to came to, play at Hutton-on-t'-Moor.

The End

Best-seller lists perform the doubtful task of giving publicity to books that are already well known. For some time, the antiquarian book trade has been crying out for a regular guide to the other end of the market where the books most in demand tend to be the hardest to come by, and therefore the slowest moving. Now, at last, we proudly bring you:

RARE BOOKS

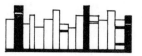

THE WORST-SELLING LIST

Twentieth Century

1. *How to Get the Most out of Your Dried Eggs*, 1943, by Wilhemina Gottsuch, HMSO. (Slight yellow stains.)

2. *The Wonderful World of French Impressionism*, 1954, printed in Romania with three plates in black and white, and text by the Central Committee of Culture. Published at 5/-, but unlikely to reach that now.

3. *The Peerless Mangle: An Instruction Booklet*, 1936, anonymous. One of the rarest of all manuals in the still undeveloped field of instruction booklets.

4. *Master Your Yo-yo!* 1938, with 2 diagrams, by Grahame Green (no relation).

5. *A Leisurely Walk through Brentwood*, by Edith and Emily Fairfax, 1956, in the 'Beauties of Essex' series.

(This is the only volume known in the series, despite the publishers' announcement of *The Billericay Nobody Knows*.)

6. *Anglo-German Cultural Exchanges*, 1939, A Full Projected List.

7. *A Hungarian-Esperanto Dictionary*, Volume 1 (Esperanto-Hungarian A–M), 1961, Budapest and Zurich. Marginal notes in (?) Swedish.

8. *Enid Blyton's Famous Five: A Marxian Analysis*, 1956, by Professor Itol Sussmayr, Centre for Literary Studies, Albania. Inscribed 'Love to Daisy, from Mummy and Daddy, on her twelfth birthday'.

9. *The Collected Poetical Works of Amy Tranter*, 1927, privately printed.

10. *So You Want to be a Dirigible Pilot?* 1928, by Captain O'Shaughnessy of the Irish Air Force.

Pre-1900

1. *The Complete Waverley Novels*, Sir Walter Scott (only 39 volumes missing).

2. *The Perfect Housekeeper*, by A Lady who Has Some Experience, 1896.

3. *The Works of Alexander Pope*, 1763, Vol 14, being 'Works by Other Hands, but Printed under Mr Pope's Name Mistakenly or Otherwise'.

4. *A Map of London*, 1880, with Westminster and Knightsbridge missing.

5. *De Natura Sciaticae*, 1781, by A Doctor: a work in Latin on bone ailments and their current treatments, all of which are disproved by the author.

6. *Who's Who, 1168,* containing only two entries: a long favourable one on Henry II, and a much shorter, less favourable one on Thomas a Becket.

7. *The Charge of the Fire Brigade*, 1867, a long comic poem printed in admiration of Lord Tennyson.

8. *The Transactions of the Historical Society of Buenos Aires*, 1897, Vol VIII, No 23.

9. *An Account of a Walking Tour of Anatolia Cut Short by the Death of the Author's Mother*, 1863, by a Gentleman.

10. *Why Man Will Never Fly: God's Will Explained*, 1881, by the Very Rev Anstruther Willesden.

CARBON PAPER.
Doesn't look much, does it?

Just a sheet of nondescript paper which dirties your hands and makes marks on your clean shirt cuffs.

Oh yes, it's very easy to make fun of carbon paper. All that effort stuffing it between your ordinary writing paper and getting it the right way round, when it's so much easier to get copies out of a photomachine. Or a word so-called processor. Or any of the magic electronic aids which are supposedly going to make your life so much happier.

And yet, you know, electricity may have run out completely by the year 1998. A recent survey showed that there is only enough natural electricity in the world to run the music centres and data processors *already manufactured* for another twenty years.[1] And how will we get copies then?

Good old-fashioned carbon paper is suddenly going to look pretty good. Completely self-powered, ecologically sound and complying with all noise abatement requirements, carbon paper may well come back into its own as early as 1989.[2] Small wonder if some firms are already reverting to a carbon paper-geared economy.[3]

Did you know that there are enough deposits of carbon existing naturally in Britain to feed the entire memorandum industry till AD 2500 at the earliest? That South Wales, Lanarkshire and parts of Geordieside are so rich in natural carbon that the landscape itself is black with thumb prints? And that over 87,000 people are still fully employed in mining the carbon or spraying its derivative on to sheets of paper? Or that the Black Type Mills Band recently came second in the Belgian Brass Championships?

Once upon a time Britain led the world in carbon paper technology. It isn't often enough remembered that Lincoln's Gettysburg Address (No 1, the Avenue, Gettysburg) was rushed round the world on British carbon paper. As was Walt Whitman's *Leaves of Grass* and Stephen Foster's *Massa's In De Coal Coal Ground.*[4]

Just for a moment, carbon paper is the poor relation of Britain's file copy industry. We admit that.[5] But we are so confident that carbon paper will come back, that we have invested over £8m in new pits in the carboniferous areas of Yorkshire and North Wales, where research teams of touch typists and coffee-break technicians have reported significant new break-throughs.

And don't forget that carbon paper dating gives much better results than any comparable method. We can tell to within a fortnight when any given letter was written. Failing which, carbon paper dating *could* fix you up with the escort of a lifetime!

But enough of words, if that is possible. If you would like to test the efficacy of carbon paper, simply write to the sponsors of this advertisement and we will send back a carbon copy of your letter by return of post, or later, if our secretaries are snowed under.

Remember. Carbon paper is not just the method of the past. It could also replace the new technology. It better had. Otherwise this ad has been a waste of money. (*Sponsored by the Carbon Paper Marketing Board and National Union of Copy Miners.*)

1. 'The Coal-Powered Cassette Recorder: A Feasibility Study', NUCM Press.
2. Carbon Paper News, Vol 2, No 11.
3. eg J. F. Wilkinson, **Black Pudding Makers of Macclesfield**.
4. Black Music Press of Washington.
5. 'We Admit That'. Booklet issued by Carbon Paper Marketing Board.

Inspector Darwin Works It Out

1982 being the International Year of Charles Darwin, we proudly bring you an extract from yet another new book.

'Thank you all for turning up so promptly.'

Inspector Charles Darwin looked round at the eight people gathered in the library. The eight people who had been present on the night Lord Garnish had died. One of them had delivered the fatal blow. For 12 chapters Darwin had been gathering, sifting and selecting evidence. Now the last chapter had arrived and it was time to present the reader with his conclusions.

'Ladies and gentlemen, I don't think you will be too shocked if I tell you that one of us here tonight is a killer.'

Those present gasped and looked uneasily at each other, all except Lady Garnish who smiled faintly and went on clutching her hip flask of brandy. She had not heard a word addressed to her for two days.

'On the night of the murder you were all engaged in a light-hearted amateur dramatic production of *La Ronde*, a comedy by a Mr Arthur Schnitzler. With some difficulty I have established all your whereabouts during this complex play, and one thing becomes clear: you all had a clear opportunity to deliver the fatal blow with the music stand. Not only that, but you all had a motive for killing his Lordship.'

Nobody moved a muscle.

'You, Sir Hugo, hated your father because he was a mean old skinflint. Lady Daphne, you had been cruelly seduced by Lord Garnish and abandoned. Mr Carstairs here could not abide Lord Garnish's adoption of the faddish phrase "No way". And so on.

'But fully to understand this death, I think we have to go back a few years. About three million to be precise. To a time when there was a struggle of survival between species of whose size and strength we can have little conception. A time when to survive at all meant defending your life and if necessary killing others with no compunction; when those who were not fit to survive were weeded out by the forces of nature.'

The company moved uneasily. Mrs Whittington voiced the thoughts of all them.

'I don't see what this has to do with Lord Garnish's death, Inspector. You're not suggesting he was killed by a maddened triceratops, are you?'

Darwin smiled.

'Not quite, Mrs Whittington. I am just saying that Lord Garnish is a perfect specimen of the kind of organism that nature discards without pity. The identity of the murderer has, as a matter of fact, been perfectly clear to me since Chapter 3. The small worm casts dropped by the body . . . the odd fossilized pebble . . . the careless failure to wipe fingerprints off the music stand—all these revealed the answer immediately.

'But my paramount consideration was that whoever did the job has hastened the process of evolution, by ridding the world of a most unworthy specimen. Some might call it murder; scientifically, it can only be called progress. That being so, I shall report to my superiors that the case has remained unsolved.'

After a stunned silence, the eight guests broke into loud cheers and chaired the modest Inspector from the room. Darwin had done it again!

The End

This is a new service for those who like classical records, but find the stuff on the best-selling classical list rather heavy going. For them, and for all those who have decided that concert music is not nearly as bad at they once thought, we present:

CLASSICAL RECORDS
THE MONSTER—SELLING LIST

1. *Placido Domingo Sings Julio Iglesias.* 'O Mein Papa', 'My Heart Belongs to Daddy' and 18 other massive hits, with the Hollywood Bowl Orchestra. (OTT 459100, £5.99, also cassette.)

2. *James Galway and His Golden Flute: Themes from Great Silent Movies.* (Mogadon PVC 495100, also on cassette, £5.99.)

3. *Placido Domingo: 'It's Easy to Tango!'* Step-by-step instructions by the king of Latin music, together with life-size foot charts, free bow-tie and souvenir booklet of Buenos Aires.

(Supertax 419500, £5.99, also in paperback.)

4. *James Galway and his Platinum Flute: Saturday Night in Old Belfast!* The knees-up records to end all knees-up records, with the lads of Murphy's Bar and the Massed Bands of the SAS. (Harp 409510, £5.99, also in bottle and can.)

5. *Sing Along with Placido Domingo!* The darling of the late-night chic opera party crowd in concert with the Royal Covent Garden Opera House audience, taking nineteen encores, cheeky devil. (Valium 001945, £5.99, also in flip-top dispenser.)

6. *James Galway and his Diamond Flute: The James Joyce Centenary Album*, with Joyce's verses read by Pam Ayres. (Harp 954100, £5.99, with many photos of Frank Delaney.)

7. *The John Williams No-Gimmick LP, Just One Guitar and No Messing About*. Honest. Well, with Guest Stars Cleo Lane, John Dankworth and Andre Previn. But otherwise no gimmicks. Backing by The Who. (Glitter 001954, £5.99, also autographed, £50.)

8. *Andre Previn and Friends, Vol 8.* Features actual live recording of Andre Previn being congratulated by his friends on success of Vols 1–7. (Ferguson 901450, £5.99, also on video.)

9. *The All-Electric HMS Pinafore.* New York cast recording of new Gilbert and Sullivan smash hit, featuring Placid Domingo and Sting, and introducing the tap-dancing of Rudolf Nureyev. (Lloyd Webber 900145, £5.99, also in mono.)

10. *James Galway and his Nuclear-Powered Flute: Tunes from the Great Commercial Jingles.* (Hovis 910054, £5.99, also in giant, economy and budget pack.)

11. *Placido Domingo sings Lullabies.* Yes, go to sleep with the Barry Manilow of opera! (Barbiturate 590104, £5.99, in vanilla, orange, or cinnamon.)

12. *The James Galway-Placido Domingo a gogo Party Album!* Dance the night away with Plac and Jim, also Stephane and Yehudi, John and Cleo, Julian and John, Andre and friends! (Parky 900154, with free sick-bag.)

O F ALL the writers whose centenaries are falling this year, I knew only two reasonably well—James Joyce and A. A. Milne. And what a contrasting pair they made: Milne, the flamboyant, fiery experimental spirit, and Joyce, the quiet suburbanite from Dublin, sitting hour after hour with his wife in the café. I myself spent several years in Paris in the 1920s running an avant-garde jazz magazine, funded mostly by the generosity of Nancy Cunard and containing mostly, if the truth be known, interviews with Nancy's black boyfriends, and that's how I got to know the two of them.

Milne it was who led most of our wildest expeditions. One night, I remember, he conceived a passion for honey and at 2 am led us all—Hemingway, Pound, the Duke of Windsor, Sylvia Beach etc—round the cafés of Paris in a lunatic search for it. At other times he would gather a gang of writers to run down to the Seine and spend hours dropping empty bottles of wine over the Pont Neuf to see which would come out first the other side, experiences which he was to use later in his fiction. What a madcap he was!

Joyce was too quiet to take part in these exploits. He would sit in the café talking, thinking, but mostly worrying.

'What's to become of a fellow like me?' he'd ask me. 'Here I am poor, half-blind, not well and altogether miserable. What could I do?'

'Be a blues singer,' I suggested. 'You've got everything! Take up the guitar and I promise to feature you in the mag. Blind Boy Joyce talks to *Blue Horizon*.'

But he would never hear of it, being too busy working on a children's book he had an idea for. That's how I remember him meeting Milne for the first time. I had arranged to meet Milne in the café—I think I was trying to persuade him to take up the trumpet—and I was already sitting with Joyce when he arrived.

Of course, both being writers, they talked straight across me. Milne apparently was engaged on a tremendous great novel, the sound of which excited Joyce a lot.

'Well,' said Milne, 'I'm trying to encapsulate the whole of human existence in just one day's activities. My hero, Christopher Robin, is setting off to find the North Pole.'

'It's been found already, if you don't mind my saying so,' commented Joyce.

'Ah, but never in the woods of Sussex, which is where my hero is concentrating his search. It's partly ironic, partly because I know Sussex better than the Arctic. Anyway, on his search he encounters various animals—tigers, donkeys, bears—oh, it's too complicated to explain, because apart from anything else I have to invent a new kind of language.'

'New kind of language?' marvelled Joyce.

'Yes,' said Milne, 'based on the way we *really* hear words, so that they come out as heffalump, woozle, haycorn, wol and so on. But tell me more about your children's book.'

'Oh, it's nothing,' said Jim Joyce. 'Just about a gang of kids who have set up camp in a Martello Tower in Dublin. Tell me more about your big novel. Have you got any you can show me?'

'I've not actually started it,' admitted Milne. 'Sometimes I feel I'm not up to a big book. Perhaps I ought to start by writing for children, something short. What's the market like?'

At that point the Duke of Windsor came in and I went over to join him, but I need hardly tell you that that casual meeting of Joyce and Milne, for which I was responsible, had a seminal effect on twentieth-century literature. I should be proud of having enabled both men to find their true identity by swapping books, but it is outweighed by crossness that they never wrote for my magazine again.

With the Duke of Windsor I had better luck, as I did manage to persuade him to take up the drums, and he became a quite useful small group drummer, even if his rhythm was a little stiff—all those military parades, I expect. He should mix much more with Americans, I told him, to get the feel of things. And so he did. It was in my presence, as a matter of fact, that he met his future wife, but that is another story.

A TEARFUL Sir Peter Parker said today that he was absolutely overwhelmed by the way ordinary members of the public had flocked to his support after British Rail had gone bankrupt. More than £15m had been sent in by fare-dodgers alone, and another £3.60 or more had been left anonymously in a local train to Leamington Spa.

'It's staggering. It's unbelievable,' said Sir Peter, tearfully brushing back an accountant last night at the appeal HQ at King's Cross. 'They haven't just sent money, they've sent thousands of sandwiches, hundreds of Scotch eggs and a whole signal box that someone took home by mistake. Loyalty on this scale makes you want to go on fighting to the bitter end, or Didcot, if that's where we have to terminate.'

Hundreds of Parker's long-term staff marched on Downing Street yesterday to present a petition to the Prime Minister, asking for British Rail to receive another government hand-out. When the front door refused to open, a small squad of experienced guards beat on it, crying: 'Come on, open up, or just push your ticket out under the door!' Later they confirmed they had been allowed inside No 10 and had tracked the Prime Minister down to a locked lavatory, but would not say whether they had received an answer.

Meanwhile, the City's attempt to put together a package to save British Rail had met with disappointing results. The package had been put together all right, but after it had been delivered to Paddington it had been lost sight of; staff claimed it had been put on the last train to Exeter, but the parcels staff at Exeter reported no such package arriving, or indeed any such train.

'It's things like this that make travelling by train the last great adventure,' a still tearful Sir Peter Parker claimed late last night as he fought to keep together the travel network he has built up from a small profitable link between Stockton and Darlington to a huge, nationwide loss-making project. 'It's marvellous to think that in this day and age you can get on the 9.10 express from Edinburgh in the morning and arrive the same evening somewhere totally unexpected.'

It still seems unthinkable to most people that British Rail could ever disappear. It has weathered so many storms already, having survived the switch-over from steam to diesel and electric, from profit to loss, and now the final transfer from rail to road and air. All through it has been Sir Peter Parker's dream to give the travelling public rail journeys at prices the Government could afford, and to that end he had invented such revolutionary devices as the Awayday Breakfast, the Single Parent in a Stress Situation Concession, York Railway Museum and Jimmy Savile OBE.

'Yes, guys and gals, it's absolutely true,' says Jimmy Savile OBE. 'From tomorrow you won't be able to travel anywhere in the country by rail, thanks to bankruptcy—and it's all totally free! How's about that?'

The receiver's first job will be to sell off the parts of British Rail for which buyers can be found, notably the lucrative Inter-City Corridor Coffee Empire and the world famous Guards Announcement Training and Elocution Centre at Doncaster. The Spanish World Cup organizers are expressing keen interest in buying the British Rail Police Force outright—no one has greater experience of British sports lovers—and the receiver says that this is the first time an entire trade union, Aslef, has ever come on to the market in mint condition, though nobody has expressed any interest whatsoever so far.

But what of Sir Peter Parker?

'We'll probably get a few bob for him too,' said a tearful receiver. 'I just hope I don't have to split him up too, and sell his knighthood off separately.'

Great Alternative Partnerships of History

No 1: Alcock and Sullivan

(The first men to fly a musical across the Atlantic to America)

Chapter One
Nearly nineteen centuries had passed since the birth of Christ and still man had not achieved his great dream of taking a musical across the Atlantic to America. It had been done the other way, of course; hardly a day passed without a New York show called *Dancing Mad* or *I'm here to Marry an English Lord* arriving in the West End. Henry James, it was rumoured, had been working on a musical for ten years and was even now engaged on cutting down the opening song, 'I'm in love with a wonderful girl, though the use of the word wonderful, as it were, must not be taken to mean anything more than a kind of sylvan beauty which, in other circumstance' from its full 36 minutes.

But nobody had managed to take an English musical to Broadway. Sandy Wilson was not even born yet.

Chapter Two.
Although Sandy Wilson was not born yet, the party was in full swing. The champagne flowed like champagne, and the Edwardian conversation glittered, as if the talkers were aware that the best remarks of their generation would die on the fields of Flanders. Flanders was not born yet, nor was Swann.

'Sir Arthur, I don't know if you've met John Alcock?'

Sullivan was dressed in full composer's gear—top hat, scarf, small carnation and inky fingers. Plain John Alcock wore a flying helmet, goggles and steely blue eyes. They looked at each other and burst into roars of laughter. It was a great working partnership at first sight.

130

Chapter Three

'You really think she'll make it?' said Sir Arthur, he looked doubtfully at the contraption of wire, wood, flats and painted scenery that they had dubbed *The Pirate of Penzance.*

'She'll do,' said John Alcock flatly. 'Since you lightened Act III it's done much better. You still insist on bringing all those constabulary chaps?'

'Absolutely.'

'Right. I'm aiming for take-off on the 13th. Conditions will be ideal—a full moon and the Shubert Theatre empty on Broadway for landing.'

Chapter Four

The 13th dawned bright and early, but the outer starboard soprano went down with Laryngitis. A replacement was hastily sent down from Drury Lane.

Chapter Five

'It's now or never,' said Sir Arthur on the 14th. 'I hear Edward German is planning to take a musical across next week.'

'The Germans are nobody's fools,' grunted John. 'Right, let's go!'

Minutes later *The Pirate of Penzance* took off and vanished into the western sky. On the lone strip below one man stood and watched the dot, shaking his fist furiously. It was the man from American Equity.

Chapter Six

'We're losing height still,' gasped Alcock.

'What?' said Sullivan.

'WE'RE LOSING HEIGHT STILL!' yelled Alcock above the howl of the baritones. 'We'll have to jettison Acts 2 and 3!'

'Never!' said Sullivan

Then it happened.

'Angels 215!' cried Alcock. And sure enough, out of the sky came a flight of angels, holding on to their bowler hats with one hand and offering thousands of pounds of backing with the other, repayable in a year or for a percentage of the box office.

'We must never tell anyone about this,' said Alcock, as the musical soared again and Sullivan handed out receipts gratefully. 'Nobody would ever believe us.'

(This is part of a new series designed to celebrate British achievement and to get turned into a lucrative TV programme. Coming soon: Flanders and Edgar.)

'One-day cricket mania is sweeping Australia...beer cans flew, drunks fought, and women bared their breasts.' *Sydney Sun*

LAST MAN IN

A modern cricket story for boys
(Sponsored by Third Man aftershave)

'Middle and leg, please,' said Jack.

'Find it your flaming self,' said the umpire.

Jack felt sick. Nine wickets down, and he was the last man in for England. There were 624 runs still to get, and only 10 minutes in which to get them. Could he do it? Jack felt sick.

He gave himself guard and looked round the field. The Australian fielders snarled back and continued throwing lager cans to each other; the dying evening sun glinted on the ring pulls which littered the outfield but the light was still good enough to read the advertisements tattooed on their chests. Jack glanced at the enormous electronic scoreboard. It said: 'Miss Australia Lager will commence her streak in five minutes time.'

'Play!' called the umpire.

The ground trembled slightly as the Australian fast bowler started his run-up. He was a tall man, heavily built but smelling elegantly of Third Man aftershave, with pistol holsters dangling on both sides. As he ran past the umpire something fell from his pocket to the ground. It looked like a bottle of Australian wine. Nuits St Bruce.

'No ball!' shrieked the umpire.

A red blur flew from the bowler's hand, struck the pitch and reared up to hit Jack on his All-Round Vision Plexiglass Space Helmet. Jack sank into unconsciousness, and moments later woke up in his comfy bed in Stevenage New Town, his teddy bear in his hand and his British Home Stores duvet on the floor, where he had kicked it in his sleep. Thank God, it had all been a dream!

'Wake up,' said the umpire, leaning over him. Jack opened his eyes. Oh my God! It was Stevenage that had been the dream. It was Sydney Cricket Ground that was real.

'623 to get, and eight more minutes, you pommy bastard,' said the umpire, not unkindly.

The fielders were shouting raucous insults at him in a foreign language now, Australian probably, and the first flakes of snow were beginning to fall. Small earth tremors had made cracks in the outfield, which would make boundaries harder to get. This time the fast bowler approached the wicket on a 500cc motor bicycle; amazingly, Jack managed to get an edge and the ball flew past extra cover.

'Run up, you chaps!' called the English captain from the pavilion steps. He was felled by a well-aimed beer barrel. But Jack and his partner were running well between the wickets, for the Australian fielders, hopelessly drunk by now, were unable to focus enough to find the ball. By the time they had run 400 runs, the stumps had been thrown down three times, but only by lager cans.

Ten minutes later, with time added on to complete the ball played, England had run all 623 runs and had won a famous victory. As Jack left the pitch he raised his bat, partly in triumph, partly to fend off the crowd who were closing in on him. Later he was given the Man of the Match title. It had never been awarded posthumously before.

The End

♥

Today is February 15, the day of St Georgia, patron saint of all those who forgot St Valentine's day. The following paid insertions have been received.

MUGWUMPS sorry I couldn't get the cash together in time for Saturday's *Times*—bank backings fell through last moment—undying love Tiggy Winkle.

MUGWUMPS no message in Saturday's *Times* from Tiggy Winkle. Does this mean all is over between you and him? Is there hope for me? Hoochie Coochie.

HOOCHIE COOCHIE you keep out of this. Tiggy Winkle.

DEVASTATED because you didn't get the Valentine message you prayed for on Saturday? Get away from it all in North Africa. Still a few two-year package holidays available from Foreign Legion Tours, tel. Morocco 657834.

ANONYMOUS Valentine cards decoded by expert handwriting authority. A few words are enough for me to give you rundown on sender's character and identity, and to advise on wisdom of pursuing relationship. In complete confidence to Graphic Labs, Slough.

LARGE STOCK of mint condition Valentine cards, unsold due to being mistakenly put on display in condolence section. Huge discounts! Buy now for next February. Box 135.

FATTY MORGANA, belle of the ball, Fatty Morgana, so wide and so tall! I beg of you, Fatty, on bended knees To listen to my impassioned pleas!—Lugworm.

TIGGY WINKLE I will not be silent. My love for Mugwumps is greater than you can ever know. It is deeper than the National Dept and wider than the Champs Elysée. It is grander than Norman St John-Stevas and finer than (I'm sorry, you have only paid enough for three similes.—Ed). Hoochie Coochie.

HOOCHIE COOCHIE you snivelling wretch, Mugwumps wouldn't touch you with a barge pole. I may be unreliable, but she loves me, warts and all. Tiggy Winkle.

TIGGY WINKLE then how come she didn't send you a Valentine message, eh? Hoochie Coochie.

FOR FORTY YEARS, Fatty, I have from afar, sung songs to you on a small guitar, Under the sun and under the moon, Always a semitone out of tune.—Lugworm

YOUR Valentine cards cleared away by an expert, also antique furniture, heirlooms etc. Just go out one evening to the theatre and we will be round in a flash. Jim, Dave and Curly.

CAN YOU BE SUED for promises made in a greetings card? Hire the experts to clear up your Valentine problems. Tutt, Graft, Hardly and Binding, solicitors of Bradford.

MUGWUMPS well, come on, woman, make your mind up. Tiggy Winkle, Hoochie Coochie.

CAN'T STOP FALLING in love? Share your problems with Romantics Anonymous. Use your new Computer Undating service, and find someone totally unsuited. It works!

AND ONE OF THE numbers that I have played, Is now number ten in the hit parade, So Fatty Morgana, you beautiful thing, Won't you come a bit closer and hear what I sing?—Lugworm.

LUGWORM you sound my kind of feller. Write to me c/o *The Times* and let's take it from there. Mugwumps.

WORLD CUP '82

Football specialist Rene McGrit looks at England's fellow group members.

IN THEIR opening group England have been drawn against France, Czechoslovakia and Kuwait, and while England supremo Ron Greenwood can heave a sigh of relief that he will not be encountering heavyweights like Brazil or West Germany just yet, he is too experienced not to know that at this stage of the competition everyone is dangerous.

'They must be good, otherwise they wouldn't be going to Spain,' he says with that classic simplicity that has endeared him to logical symbolists the world over.

Czechoslovakia are perhaps the chief threat. This country of lovely rolling hills and woods is also a land renowned for its skilled industry, and it was a mixture of skill and industry that deservedly brought Czechoslovakia the European crown in recent years. Although they have faded slightly since then, these wily East Europeans have a proud tradition to draw on; they may no longer have stars like (fill from cuttings), but they are still a force to be reckoned with.

If any country presents a danger to England, it must be France. This land of *cuisine* and *haute couture* is no less famous for its age-old artistry, and their 1978 World Cup artists provided a few shocks in Argentina, where they were desperately unlucky to lose to (Austria 2-1, was it? Look it up for me, could you?). They may have gone through a quiet patch since then, but these mercurial Gallic warriors can never be taken for granted, and England will have all their work cut out to keep them at bay.

Of all the dark horses, Kuwait present perhaps the fiercest challenge. This Arab sheikhdom of rolling sand dunes and fierce sunshine is equally a land of oil and money, and wise investment and coaching have brought them to the top of their strongly contested 1982 World Cup group. Whether they can keep up that kind of momentum remains to be seen. We may as yet be unfamiliar with their star names such as (look out any of the Kuwaiti team, could you, love? Make up a few if necessary), but come summer the England squad will be treating these twinkle-toed sons of Allah with a great deal of respect.

As there don't seem to be any other teams in this group, except England, we should remind ourselves that Greenwood's men are poised on the brink of great things. At club level we have never been stronger, and it is only a matter of time before we come good nationally as well.

There seems no reason why the birthplace of football should not once again show the rest of the world how to play, and if we can't beat the Czechs, who were lucky to scrape through against Wales, a bunch of fairy-footed Frenchmen and a band of Bedouin bandits who don't even use knives and forks, then my name's not Rene McGrit. God, I'm so sick and tired of having to apologize for England being taken to the cleaners by pooftahs like the Swiss and Norwegians, that if I have to do it again I'm going to jack the whole thing in and take up drinking seriously. Meanwhile, it's worth remembering that World Cup football is a funny game, and the most unlikely results can occur, as when mighty Scotland were toppled by little-fancied Peru four years ago. I don't see that happening again, though, and I strongly fancy my home country to go marching through against any opposition this time. Forget the plodders of England, forget the Irish amateurs, and keep your eyes on our 11 wee Scottish heroes who, I promise you, will run rings round any Dagoes or Russkies sent against us.

As long as we avoid our national habit of taking things for granted, I reckon the World Cup is as good as in the bag for us, and on Cup Final night I'll be out there in the streets of wherever it is waving my scarf with the tartan army. Watch out, everyone! Article ends.

(I'll be at this phone number till closing time, pet, if there are any queries. Just check to see I've got England in the right group, would you? Change names if necessary. And if the sports editor is snooping around, make sure the bottle's locked up in my desk. Thanks, hen.)

'IT MAY be necessary to withdraw the Inter-City Saver facility during the period of the papal visit.'
(From a new British Rail low fares brochure.)

I wonder what the word 'save' means to you. I know what it means to me. It means so very many different things. When Pat

Jennings pushes a hard shot round the upright, we say he has 'saved' the goal. We can 'save' a historic station or signal box for the nation. Or we can cut out the top of a washing powder packet (if we've got jolly tough scissors!) and buy a return ticket to Redruth for only 50p, as long as we travel after 10 am, but not on Fridays.

All this can be called saving.

But sometimes we also mean a more important sense—to *rescue* something. When the passengers of a crashed aircraft are found unhurt on a hillside, or a man is plucked from the sea by a helicopter, we say that they have been *saved*. I often think, you know, that life is a bit like a dinghy sailing trip—one moment everything seems so smooth and calm, the next you're washing around in the briny. And at moments like this we feel, don't we, that it would be safer to travel by train? And that, perhaps, we should turn for guidance to a higher authority.

That is why we have now instituted the Inter-City Saver facility on many main line trains. Beside your seat you should find a copy of the Gideon Bible. Towards the middle of the train, next to the buffet, and eventually replacing it altogether, you will find a small meditation area, which we call Traveller's Prayer. And on many trains there will be a roving minister who will be delighted to help you. So if you hear an announcement beginning 'This is your padre speaking,' don't be alarmed. Be of good cheer! He is sitting in what we call the God's van, ready to help you.

This is not the first time that there has been an Inter-City Saver facility. In the Bible we read that Paul saw the light of truth while en route from Jerusalem to Damascus, and this is the tradition that we are trying to maintain. For life, I think sometimes, is like an Inter-City trip; some of us are chosen to travel first class with plenty of room for our newspapers, some of us are called to sit in the surprisingly comfortable second class coaches of life while others may have to sit on their suitcases in life's corridor.

Wherever we are in our Inter-City progress, I hope we can all spare a thought for the more unfortunate—for those forced to travel in from Shenfield or Gidea Park, for instance—and your padre may well organize a small collection for those in peril on the Eastern Region. I often find it useful in adversity to remember the words of our patron, Jimmy Savile OBE:

'How's about that, guys and gals!'

I wonder what he means by that? To me, it is a message of hope and encouragement. The railway timetable, you know, is not unlike the Bible; both of them announce a programme of perfection to which we can very seldom attain. But unless we can travel with the hope of arrival before us, then it is hardly worth travelling at all. 'We regret the late arrival', you sometimes hear people say. Well, yes, life is full of regrets, but we must always look forward—let us not be one of life's platform-ticket-holders, too frightened to go on the great journey.

We do not, of course, claim to have a monopoly of the truth at British Rail and it may prove wise to withdraw our Inter-City Saver facility during the Pope's visit. But we shall be back again afterwards, and I look forward perhaps to meeting you all then. Remember, all faiths are welcome on British Rail, as long as you hold a valid ticket or travelling permit.

Now here are the main points of the sermon again.

The Men from Sotheby's!

A Classic Tale of Adventure

'Miss Harriet van Gogh?'

The woman who opened the door of the neat Belgian suburban house was about fifty and clearly unmarried, except perhaps to the four or five cats who dawdled round her feet. She looked up anxiously at the tall young man who addressed her and agreed that she was.

'And the last surviving relative of the great painter, Vincent?'

'Yes, monsieur. But if you are from the newspapers, I am afraid I have very little to tell you. He was only a great-great uncle.'

The young man smiled.

'No, I am not from the press. I am no great friend of the press, indeed. I work for Sotheby's, the great art sellers of London, and we have just sold one of Vincent's paintings for £800,000.'

'That is good, monsieur, but I don't see...'

'We have also just instituted a rule that after each sale the artist must pay 10 per cent of the price. Or, if the artist is dead, his estate or family.'

As the information sank in, Miss van Gogh looked incredulous.

'But that is monstrously unfair!'

'Not at all, mamselle. The buyer pays 10 per cent, the seller pays 10 per cent—why not the artist too? Why, even the auctioneers pay 10 per cent!'

'You mean, your firm pays *itself*?'

'No, no. The auctioneer, the man conducting the auction, pays us 10 per cent of his commission each time he bangs his gavel. Of course, it is not his gavel. We insist he rents it from us.'

'I have never heard anything so ridiculous in my life. Please go away.'

The young man's smile went thin but did not vanish.

'You may have cause to regret your obduracy, mamselle.'

Jean-Luc Rodin tossed the newspaper away impatiently. What rubbish they printed these days. Explosion in Belgian Suburb—Many Cats Feared Dead, indeed! He was about to reach for some work when his secretary buzzed him.

'That man from London is here again.'

'Ah, send him in.'

The tall young man came in and shook hands with Jean-Luc.

'Any luck, M Rodin?'

'Yes, I have, I have found someone who is a closer surviving relative of the great sculptor than I am. She is a widow living in the Dordogne. Here is her name and address. But you must hurry, for she is old.'

'In that case,' said the young man, 'I shall look forward to meeting you again soon, and doing business with you.'

No, you will not, thought Rodin, for when you come back I shall be living elsewhere under an assumed name.

The Post-Impressionist School still thrives in a large building in the Avenue de Neuilly, but when the British businessman with the moustache and briefcase knocked at its front door, he found it tight locked. Eventually, through a small grille, a voice said: 'Are you from Sotheby's?'

'Certainly not,' said the man briskly.

'Do you swear that you have no connexion of any sort with the auction house of that name and its accursed gang?'

'I swear.'

The door was gradually unlocked. When it finally swung open, the man stepped quickly inside and presented a card.

'Christie's of London,' he said. The concierge fainted.

The island of Sicily lay peaceful in the sunshine. Nobody stirred. This was partly because it was siesta time. More important, it was because the day before there had been a big sale of Sicilian art at Sotheby's, and the Mafia had taken to the hills in fear.

'The millionaire businessman who tried to take over the street ice cream, hot dog and soft drink campaign with a reign of terror was jailed for four years at the Old Bailey . . . He forced other operators out of business by intimidation, ramming their vans and beating people up . . . The racketeers charge as much as £1.50 for an ice cream.' *The Standard.*

JACK THE RIPPLE

It was a soft, creamy dawn over London. Chocolate whorls of cloud decorated the horizon while starlings hung stiffly in the trees like mint chips on a vanilla cornet. With his foot, Inspector Wafer of the Yard stirred the glowing embers of what had once been an ice cream van.

'It's happened at last, Jack,' he said. 'The Ice Cream War has broken out.'

Sergeant Jack Coupe looked impressed.

'What do we do now?'

Wafer looked nonplussed for a moment. Then his face brightened.

'I know,' he said. 'We'll form an Ice Cream Squad.'

Night. Hendon. The sky, soft-dark as a chocolate mousse, hung over the rooftops. The chimneys, like flake bars, stuck up into it. Everything was quiet, except for the sound of a far-off cornet.

Suddenly round a corner, lights blazing, bells ringing, came an ice cream van at 75 mph. It crashed right into the police barrier.

'All right,' said Superintendant Walls heavily into the driver's window. 'We've got you on 15 different counts. Exceeding the speed limit, not paying copyright on *Teddy Bears Picnic*, wiping out the 'Lucky' Cassata gang . . .'

The driver pushed a police ID card at him.

'Wafer, Ice Cream Squad,' he said.

The Neopolitan dusk went down over the South Kensington museum complex, green, then pink, then white. Inspector Wafer, dressed uncomfortably as a lollipop lady, nudged Jack Coupe, resplendent as a traffic warden.

'That's him.'

He nodded at the Mr Freezy van parked ostentatiously outside the Natural Seismological Museum. The man inside was six foot four, with scars on both cheeks, a cauliflower ear and raspberry bloodstains on his white overalls.

'That's who?' said Jack, puzzled.

'He's only a small operator,' said Wafer, 'but he'll lead us to the big man. You cover the back, I'll go in the front.'

Minutes later the big man was sweating, ground remorselessly down by the sheer tedium of the police questioning.

'OK, OK,' he said. 'I'll tell you who the big man is.'

Wafer hit him once more for luck. Inside the Seismological Museum they registered force three on the Richter Scale.

'Jack the Ripple,' said Wafer. 'That's the man we're after. Somewhere in London there is hundreds of tons of this soft white substance, bringing misery to the addicts who are dependent on this vile trade. But I'll devote the rest of my life if necessary to bringing down this gang of devils in human form!'

'Bit melodramatic, isn't it, sir?' said Jack.

'Sorry,' said Wafer. 'I keep thinking the BBC cameras are still here.'

A lemon-yellow sun shone tartly over London. A rum flavour arose from somewhere. Far off, a group of pecans huddled disconsolately in London Zoo. In Hyde Park a five foot nine schoolboy asked the man in the van for a choc ice.

'That will be £4.60 plus VAT, sonny,' said the vendor.

Inspector Wafer pulled off his cap, blazer, satchel and pebble glasses.

'I am Inspector Wafer of the Ice Cream Squad,' he said.

The vendor pulled off his false nose, wig, ears and dark glasses.

'Sergeant Coupe, I'm afraid, sir,' he said.

In the House of Commons Sir Hector Vanilla, Tory MP for Bournville, South, and elected member for the ice cream trade, got to his feet. 'May I ask the Home Secretary what progress he has to announce in the Jack the Ripple case?'

The Home Secretary got heavily to his feet. 'The police are

looking into every angle of this case and have reason to believe that it has affected even the highest in the land. More than that I cannot say at present.'

The Speaker rang his bell.

'We'll take a short break there, I think,' he said. 'While we do so, I will come among you selling wafers, cornets, choc bars and drinks on a stick.'

To be continued

Nineteen eighty-two being, as you know the Year of Charles Darwin, almost every conceivable celebration was planned except an appearance by Charles Darwin on the Michael Parkinson Show. We put that right, with these exclusive transcripts.

Parkinson: My guest this evening is someone who has done more to change the history of mankind than anyone who has ever been on this show. I spent most of my youth in Barnsley Public Library poring over his works, and it has always been my greatest ambition to meet him and ask him what they mean. Ladies and gentlemen—Charles Darwin!

(*Stupendous ovation. Darwin comes down the grand staircase and sits in the right chair.*)

Parkinson: Super. Now, Charles, in a moment I'll be asking you to play a piano duet with Yehudi Menuhim or perhaps do a few steps with Lionel Blair, but first let me ask you about the book you've got out this month.

Darwin: It's called *The Origin of The Species* and it's out in paperback this month.

Parkinson: Could you very briefly sum up the theory of the book for those in the audience who may not have had a chance to read it yet?

Darwin: Certainly, Mr Parkinson. I am trying to say that the available evidence tends to suggest that the natural world is governed by a set of laws which favour species which adapt to their environment, or in other words...

Parkinson: Or in other words that the Book of Genesis is as dead as mutton?

Darwin: Yes, I suppose you could...

142

Parkinson: Amazing. I don't think I'm betraying any secrets if I say that you are also featured on our new postage stamps, together with what looks like two glove puppets.

Darwin: Yes. This was an idea of my publisher, who has arranged a television children's series for me, in which with the help of Tommy the Turtle and Tristan the Tortoise I try to explain why one of them is doomed to extinction before the series ends.

Parkinson: Magic. You've done a lot of work with animals, haven't you? You must have had a good many hilarious experiences with them.

Darwin: Oh yes. (*Pause.*)

Parkinson: Could you tell us one?

Darwin: Well, I remember being very excited to find on the Galapagos Islands a kind of large terrapin which was significantly different from anything on the mainland. There was, as far as I could observe, only one of its kind in existence, so of course I recorded its every move. But one day it had vanished completely. It simply wasn't there. It couldn't have swum away, as it was incapable of swimming, and it couldn't have flown for similar reasons, nor did it have any natural enemies on the island. When my small team and I met for the evening meal I put the problem to them, and none of us could think of a possible explanation. Except, curiously, our Chilean cook, Garcia.

Parkinson: And that was?

Darwin: Quite simple. We had just eaten it.

Parkinson: So you are responsible personally for the extinction of an entire line of evolution?

Darwin: Yes. It tasted very good, though, so it was probably justified.

Parkinson: I think I'm right in saying that that recipe, suitably adapted for any kind of turtle, is featured in a book you have coming out next month?

Darwin: Yes, *Charles Darwin's Evolutionary Cookbook*. It's got such mouth-watering ideas as Galapagos Gazpacho, Finch Pie and Primordial Soup, and many others.

Parkinson: Wonderful. I know that worms have played a very large part in your work. Will your book have any recipes for . . . ?

Darwin: No, I'm afraid not, but I have been working closely with Andrew Lloyd-Webber on a new musical to be called Worms, so the research will not be wasted.

Parkinson: Magic. In a moment we'll be talking to James Joyce, and I can promise that he'll have some very good new Irish jokes for you, but meanwhile—Charles Darwin, thank you.

Darwin: My pleasure. (*Stupendous ovation, etc.*)

Once upon a time there was a princess who lived in a cold country a long way from here. She went hunting one day with the court, as princesses and courts are wont to do, but caught nothing all day. Towards evening she became separated from the rest of the hunters and, as she was riding through the woods towards the sound of their voices, suddenly found herself face to face with an enormous stag. Overjoyed, she raised her rifle to dispatch him.

'You're not really going to shoot me, are you?' said the stag. 'I didn't think people did that any more.'

'Good heavens,' said the princess. 'I've never met a talking stag before.'

'Well, come to that,' said the deer, 'I've never met princesses who could string more than three or four words together without the greatest difficulty. Something to do with inbreeding, I expect.'

'Then it will come as something of a final privilege to be shot by an articulate princess.'

She raised her gun again. The stag backed away.

'Your Highness, consider how wrong it would be for you to shoot me. I beg you to rethink your position before you do this terrible thing.'

'I'm not exactly surprised to find you in the anti-hunting lobby, you know.'

'Oh, I'm not against hunting,' said the stag. 'We all hunt, one way and another. And in any case, if I don't die a painful death from a bullet, I am sure to die even more painfully of exposure, or a broken leg, on some cold and draughty hillside. No, I was thinking of you and how terrible it will be for you. Things have changed now, you know, and you can't even shoot a rabbit without raising an enormous protest. Kill me, and you will become the most unpopular princess in the kingdom.'

'But I always went hunting before I became a princess, and nobody ever complained.'

'Good heavens, girl, do you know *nothing* about the media?' cried the stag. 'It's *now* that you have to be careful. I can see the headlines already. The Killer Princess. Blood on the Royal Hands.'

'Piffle,' said the princess. 'They like me.'

'They like me better,' said the stag. 'I may be totally without practical function but I am very decorative and my picture hangs on every wall in the land.'

'I know the feeling,' said the princess. 'Gets you down, doesn't it?'

'I'm glad we agree', said the stag. 'Now put that wretched

gun away.'

Just then a magnificent figure clad in the most wonderful costume galloped into the glade and came to a halt beside them.

'Whatever have we got here?' said the stag. 'Does it play in a group?'

'No,' said the princess. 'This is the Palace Spokesman'.

'Then I am in very deep trouble,' said the stag. 'This man can explain away absolutely anything. I have a feeling that I am for it.'

And he was.

THE GRAND finals of the Junk Food Expert of the Year contest were held yesterday at the Pork Scratchings motorway service area on the M11.

To get to the finals, contestants had to show considerable knowledge of all the modern forms of takeaway food, under blind-fold conditions. Only one person was disqualified for eating his blindfold. Takeaway food is, of course, nothing but a combination of unidentifiable meat and an indigestible starch wrapping, but it may take many shapes—pizza, doner kebab, hamburger, ham sandwich or savoury croissant. Extra marks were given for knowing the medical treatment involved for each.

For the finals, it was decided to make the contestants undergo the supreme junk food test: identifying potato crisps by taste alone.

To begin with the six finalists were handed a bowl of roast chicken-flavoured crisps. This was identified by four of them as Marmite-flavoured crisps, by one as cheese 'n' onion, and by the other as devilled ham. All six were correct, as, of course, all these crisps are identical.

For the next round, all contestants received plain salted crisps. Five of them correctly identified them. The sixth named them as monosodium glutamate-flavoured crisps. After some hestitation, he was given extra marks.

Moving on to slightly trickier territory, the contestants were now handed helpings of prawn-cocktail-with-advocado-mix crisps. These were unanimously named by all six as left-over shrimp shells. No marks were awarded.

To make things even harder, blindfolds were now put on the finalists and they were made to sample small pieces of salted crispy Cellophane. Four of them named these as Marmite-flavoured crisps, one as cheese 'n' onion and the other as devilled ham. Full marks were given in each case.

At this stage in the proceedings the leader was 18-year-old Gary Stubbs, an unemployed pop star from Battersea, who claims to have the largest collection of different crisps in the world (53), including the very rare fillet steak 'n' asparagus crisps which Harrods tried to market for a while.

Now each of the six was handed a glass of brown, fizzy liquid. This was identified variously as cough mixture, carbonated coffee, water from the Thames and 'diluted essence of rusty Ford Cortina'. However, it was then explained that this was not part of the contest and was simply a cola drink provided to wash down the saltiness of the crisps.

Back to the contest proper, each contestant now received a small dish of crunchy white powder which three finalists named as salt, one identified as roast-chicken-flavoured salt, one singled out as roast-chicken-'n'-sage-and-onion-stuffing-flavoured salt, and which only Gary Stubbs correctly recognized as pure cocaine.

It was in the final blindfold round that Stubbs ran away with the title. Each finalists was handed a packet of crisps which he had to identify solely by feeling the contents through the packet. Most of the panellists thought the packet contained either broken bits of streaky bacon frazzle or chunky cheddar chip sticks; only Stubbs correctly guessed that the packet contained unexpected quantities of nuts and bolts for which the company apologizes profusely—we have no idea how this came to pass and hope you will accept the enclosed crate of our new tomato-ketchup-and-brown-sauce-table-cloth-stain-flavoured crisps in recompense, J. Fothergill, Sales Manager.

For winning the title of Junk Food Expert 1982, Gary Stubbs was presented with a bronze replica of a crumpled cardboard box, a year's supply of salt in blue paper sachets and a kilt with the McDonald's tartan.

Like any able-bodied journalist, I am busy working on a book about Princess Diana. It will be called the *Princess Diana Cook Book* and should make me a fortune—I only wish I could pass on some of the money to her, but delicacy forbids.

Unfortunately, like many experts on Princess Diana, I have not had the benefit of actually meeting her, so my recipes at the moment are somewhat restricted to obvious items like Quick Venison Dinner for 500, Brown Windsor Soup, Buckingham 'n' Veal Pie, etc. With only enough ideas to fill 20 pages, I was enormously relieved therefore to read in *The Times* on Monday the following item:—

'The Prince of Wales bought a 10p tin of baked beans and a mango for £1.50 at a school fair in Brixton, south London, on Saturday and told pupils: "The Princess loves them". '

Armed with this information I have already devised, tested and perfected an enormous amount of new recipes, of which the following are a tiny selection.

Beans and Mango on Toast
1 tin of baked beans
1 mango
1 slice of bread

A personal favourite of the Princess's, this is a tasty variation on the more conventional beans on toast. Grill the bread lightly on both sides. Meanwhile, warm the beans gently in a pan and cut the peeled mango into dice. Pour the beans over the toast, add the mango chunks and serve immediately. Enough for one, or for two, if one is not very hungry.

Glazed Roast Chicken, Brixton Style
2 tins baked beans
2-3 mangoes
1 roasting chicken

A wonderful new way to make roast chicken exotically different. Simply stuff the chicken with as many beans as possible (you may have to sew up the entrance to prevent bean overspill) and roast in the normal way. The tomato-based sauce from the beans will mingle with the chicken juices to make a delicious gunge. Half an hour before serving, place strips of mango across the chicken, then baste frequently. A good mango costs anything from £1.50 at a Brixton school fair down to 80p at Harrods.

Veal, Yam and Egg Pie

This is made in exactly the same way as veal, ham and egg pie, with yams for ham. It is absolutely delicious as part of a Norfolk picnic. As a snack, it is ideal for that quick helicopter trip or boring tour of a factory, while on a Highland fishing expedition a block of veal, yam and egg pie makes very good bait, or would stun a trout with one blow.

Serve with cold beans and mangoes.

Caribbean Sauce
10-12 oz beans
mangoes cut small
seasoning

If, like me, you often find yourself with lots of left-over beans and mangoes, here is a handy tip for using them up. Put the beans in the liquidizer and make them into a purée. Add the mango bits and amalgamate them with the bean purée till you have a wonderfully maroon mixture tinged with green. Leave for an hour or so until it is beginning to set, then simply stuff it into the crevice, wall cracks or masonry fault that needs treating. When dry, it can be sanded and painted. It's also perfect for plastering, draught-proofing windows or hand-thrown pottery.

Seasoning can be omitted, if preferred.

M ANY READERS who enjoyed making pancakes this last Shrove Tuesday have written to ask me if there are any other days in the year they can look forward to, as their diaries seem to mark only Bank holidays in Scotland. Yes, certainly there are—in fact every day can be a holiday of some kind if you know your days properly.

Here are just a few of those available.

Placido Domingo. Literally, gloomy Sunday. A Mediterranean custom of going to church on Sunday morning, then wheeling out little old ladies in black dresses for a walk before Sunday lunch, which is traditionally devoted to family quarrels. In the afternoon we see Violetta, the wronged sweetheart, return to stab Esteban through the heart for his treachery, though she is to learn in Act IV that he had only done it to protect his friend Rodrigo. In the grand finale the whole family goes out to a local restaurant for dinner and all the children fall asleep at the table.

Stormy Monday. A black American festival, as commemorated in the old blues of the same name. 'They call it stormy Monday, but Tuesday's just as bad; yeah, they call it stormy Monday, but Tuesday's just as bad.' It is a lament by American blacks for all the time spent fruitlessly repeating the first lines of blues verses—time which, if properly used, could have advanced the cause of black Americans by 10 years, and there might now be American soul artistes on the moon.

Mardi Gras. 'Fat Tuesday.' The day, in France, on which all addicts of Cuisine Minceur can have a relapse from their good habits and eat as much grease as possible. In New Orleans (Nouvelle Orleans) it means something rather different (quelque chose de different) and the bands come out and play loud music on Mardi Gras (Fats Domino Placido).

Sheffield Wednesday. A good old British custom celebrated once every 40 years. On Sheffield Wednesday all the inhabitants of Sheffield come out dressed in feathers and motley garb, in an attempt to get Brian Clough to come and manage one of their football teams. There is no known cure. (Also, **Ash Wednesday**, the day on which it is traditional to give up smoking for Lent.)

Maundy Thursday. A strange relic of medieval times, when calendars were so unsure that no one quite knew if it was Monday or Thursday, and loyal subjects were given the choice. Other little known examples are Wembley Friday, Sundry Tuesday, Thirsty Saturday and Pineapple Sundae.

Long Good Friday. The First Law of Chronology states that 'weekends expand to fill available work-time' and Friday looks like being the next victim. Already Friday lunch-time starts at about 12 and ends about 3. People are starting to think that it is hardly worth going back to the office at 3. Traffic jams to the country are starting at about 2 on Friday afternoons. Hence the long good Friday. (Also **Nancy Friday:** the day in the US on which gays are allowed to do anything, and I mean *anything*. Well, for gosh sakes.)

Saturday Night Fever. Anthropologists have noticed that almost every tribe on earth suffers from the belief that something exciting will happen on Saturday night if only one dresses up colourfully and stays up late. (Television companies enjoy the same delusion.) Science can find no factual evidence for this belief, but then, when did you last find a scientist out having a good time on Saturday night? Well, then. Personally, I don't think you can beat roaming the streets at 1 am on a Sunday morning, looking for a non-existent taxi home in the rain, trying to remember the names of the people with you and being rather aware that five years ago you would probably have enjoyed all this. Well, then.

Today's Profile: Prince Nigel, the Dempster Royal.

Prince Nigel knew from a very early age that he was different from other people, and that he was destined to be a man apart. In his diary at the age of five he wrote: 'I saw daddy with a ladie today.' At the age of 10 he rang his headmaster to ask him to confirm or deny the rumours. He started his 'O' level essay on Elizabeth I: 'It was no secret that playboy courtier Duke of Essex had been squiring the Queen around the night spots of London, but sources close to the romantic couple were adamant that wedding bells were not about to ring . . . '

He was a man marked, if ever man was marked, to be Dempster Royal. (This is the Court post of social journal-writer. Dempster comes from an old form of 'deem'; the motto of the post is: 'If I deem it to be true, then it *is* true.') At the moment he is at the height of his powers. Yet, say his friends, Prince Nigel is not a happy man.

In his lonely and isolated position, he has always been subject to a great deal of malicious and uninformed criticism by the British press; today that chorus of disapproval has, if anything, increased. Yet by tradition Prince Nigel cannot answer his critics back and must suffer in silence.

'Some of the things they've been saying about Nigel are really awful,' says friend the Hon Magenta ffolkes-Vagen. 'Gosh, I mean, like they say he mixes with grand people all the time and doesn't know about real life. That he gets a great deal of money for not doing what you or I would call work. Even that his undoubted talents have been wasted in a frivolous life. Awful things like that. They may well be true, but it's awful to say them.'

Slightly less than average height, with a ready smile on his lips, some dark hair on top of his head and an ear either side, Nigel has a well-nigh perfect public image. As he moves among his people, nobody is better than he is at putting them at ease and asking the right questions, such as Who's she going out with at the moment? and Can I quote you on that? To people who provide the right answers he is more than generous. His life is full of exhausting official engagements, too—always attending the opening of new restaurants, new cocktail bars, new discos.

Yet behind the brave smile and the half-raised eyebrow (the result of an accident while out hunting a story) you can sense the sadness. It is no secret that Nigel's relationship with his legal partner, the *Daily Mail,* is an on-off affair and that they have lived apart for weeks at a time, with rancorous bickering between them.

Nor is it unknown that Prince Nigel is conducting an affair with *Private Eye,* with whom he has been in love for some time. This sort of double life can cause stress even to someone as resilient as him, especially as *Private Eye* is not, frankly, the sort of partner that a lot of people would wish for our Prince.

What Prince Nigel's inner feelings are, we cannot be sure. But there is a clue in something he said very early on in his career. 'Yes, of course I am aware of the uninformed things I have sometimes written about people. But I can assure you I no longer read any of it.'

A S THE women's movement has often pointed out, there are far too many great men in history and far too few great women. To help get things into the proper focus we offer potted biographies of some forgotten great women.

Judith Iscariot (BC ?-AD ?). The disciple we don't talk about. In her favour, she must have suffered very much from being the token woman in a male-dominated political lobby group.

Ivy the Terrible (1530-1584). Empress of Russia, remembered for her legendary bad temper. Whenever the enemies of Russia gathered, she would fly into the most tremendous rage, my dear, and they would simply fly before her. After a while she got the idea that this was the solution for all problems and flew into the most awful tantrums with the friends of Russia as well, until during the last few years of her life nobody would speak to her at all. Occasionally she would have lucid friendly moments and is remembered for the remark: 'See what the boyars in the back room will have'. She was a great empress, but impossible.

Emily Zola (1840–1901). Feminist novelist. In her early years of poverty she conceived the vast scientific theory that everything was men's fault, and wrote a vast series of novels to prove it. To her great chagrin, it proved immensely popular with men, especially her novel about battered wives *L'Assommoir* (from the French word 'assommer'—to knock down). She hit back with her outspoken open letter 'J'accuse' which put forward the theory that men were to blame for everything and for Dreyfus being sent to

Devilperson's Island. In the ensuing fuss she had to flee to England for 11 months, though inexplicably no play has been written about this by Christopher Hampton. After her death in 1902 she was given a state funeral, though by men.

Florence of Arabia (1888–1935). The first great female fashion correspondent. A total unknown at the age of 26, she was lucky enough to be caught by the outbreak of the First War in Arabia, where she had been trying to popularize the Crusader look (simple white tunic with a red cross). But as soon as she discovered the long flowing robes of the Arabs, she knew that this was *the* look for her. She made many daring sorties behind enemy lines to find out what the Arabs were wearing this season, until—as far as both Arabs and British were concerned—she was *the* fashionable leader.

In 1917 she was captured by the Turks and underwent an unexplained humilating experience; experts now think she was mortified to be taken by them for a man. After the war her fame was such that she sought to change identity by entering the WRAF under the pseudonym of Rose. She was discovered and later went into the Women's Tank Corps as TE Shirt, where she became mad about motor bike gear. She died in 1935 and is now remembered for her immense book on night-wear, the Seven Pillows of Wisdom.

Charmaine Mao (1893–1978). The greatest film star China has ever produced, who had more comebacks that Frank Sinatra. In the 1920s, as a young girl, Charmaine learnt to her chagrin that the only way to get into Chinese films was to be Chiang Kai Shek's mistress. Too proud and too ugly to stoop to such depths, she set up her own studios in the countryside and in 1935 produced *The Long March*, the epic film which made her name. After making serious dramas for 20 years, she suddenly surprised everyone in the 1950s by making a succession of comedies such as *The Great Leap Forwards, The Great Leap Backwards,* and *The Great Leap into the Middle of Nowhere*. After *The Cultural Revolution* in 1966, a box office failure, she was thought to be finished, but her last film, a frothy comedy called *Let's Not be Nasty to the Yankees*, has set new trends ever since.

'Frank' Lindy Roosevelt (1893–1945). Of all the women who have shone so brightly in American public life—Olivia Wendy Holmes, Linda Baines Johnson, Adelaide Stevenson—none has had a lustre greater than that of Lindy Roosevelt, nicknamed 'Frank' because of her habit of speaking her mind. She told the American public what she thought of it, she told Churchill what she thought of him and she told Stalin what she thought of him. It is not known if she told Hitler what she thought of him, but the message must have been pretty clear.

When not in public life, she was an avid poker player and always told her fellow players what she thought of them; if there was any suspicion of cheating, her cry of 'A new deal!' was always heard. At her death it was generally agreed that the world had lost a great woman, and a sigh of relief was heard.

Doris Karloff (1902–1971). Real name Bess Pratt, she moved to Hollywood early in her career as a film actress, started to specialize in horror roles and became well known as a sort of female Bette Davies. Her great passion in life, though, was hockey, a game unknown in America, and she started the Hollywood Girls' Hockey Club along with Evelyn Waugh and Sue Aubrey Smith. It still remains there, an outpost of very English tea and biscuits.

Dawn Bradman (1912–   ). The golden girl of Australian sport; need we say more?

TO COMMEMORATE the visit of His Holiness Pope John Paul II to Great Britain, Moreover Enterprises Ltd proudly announce the creation of a special Papal Radio Cassette Recorder.

Crafted from Italian mahogany, the casket containing this jewelled piece of machinery has been exclusively designed for us by Signore Marco McCormacki, the Papal Publicist-Designate to the Court of St James's.

The on/off knob of this hand-finished piece of antique technology has been tool-carved from real imitation ivorette, individually copied from genuine-type elephant tusks.

It costs only £4,600.

The Papal Radio Cassette Recorder will wake you in the morning at any pre-set time, God willing, with messages recorded in Polish or Latin by hand-chosen members of the Vatican Choir.

If you should fail to wake within 10 minutes, a snooze device will come into operation—a silver-gilt effigy of a Swiss Guard will emerge from the recorder and strike you on the head with a genuine model of a halberd.

Should you still fail to wake, a personal recorded message from the Pope will command you to be up and about, at the risk of damnation.

It costs only £4,600.

The design of this holy memento of the Papal Visit to Britain has been approved of by the Papal Visit Dignity and Respectability Testing Centre, Slough.

ONLY 500,000 OF THESE PAPAL RADIO CASSETTE RECORDERS ARE BEING MADE.

Every one has a brand new feature, never before used on a cassette system: the Built-In Two-way Confessional Unit.

If you will not have time to go to Confession during the day, you simply record your peccadilloes through a miniature ornate grill (based on a medieval design in Padua) on to a cassette, and drop the tape off at church or post it to your priest.

He will superimpose his responses on the tape (if he too has a Papal Visit Radio Cassette Recorder) and return it to you.

It costs only £9,200—one for you and one for your priest.

Another exclusive device is the Plainsong Sleep Control, which will give you up to an hour of medieval chanting as you go to sleep and then switch off—or you may, if you wish, have the Pope wishing you good night in six languages, followed by silence.

This is also the first radio cassette recorder with a Reverent Meditation Condition Control; to produce a tranquil calm in which to meditate, you simply pull the plug from the wall.

And if, however unlikely, anything should go wrong with the Papal Visit Radio Cassette Recorder, a puff of white smoke will be emitted to signify you need a new one.

It is only £4,600.

Make your cheque payable to Moreover Papal Account, Zurich, and send to this column.

Remember: this offer *must* close when all sets have been sold.

MOTORWAY NEWS

THE SLOW lane of the M4 between exits 7 and 9 is temporarily closed to allow practice sessions by the British Olympic long-distance roller-skating team.

Drivers proceeding east on the M2 towards Dover are asked not to use the hard shoulder between Chatham and Sittingbourne, as it is under cultivation by the police for mushrooms.

The roadworks which have been on the M1 near Newport Pagnell since 1973 have now been removed after being purchased by Sir Roy Strong for his new exhibition at the Victoria and Albert Museum, 'Up the M!'.

Fierce crosswinds may be expected between juggernauts 21 and 22 on the M6 in Cumbria.

A new half-mile stretch of the A12 (M) is to be opened tomorrow by the Under-Secretary of State for Motorways and closed for repairs again on Thursday.

Telephones along the M4 in Wales are temporarily out of action during conversion for Welsh-speaking use only; postboxes will continue to take letters in both languages.

Drivers planning to go to Manchester via the M1 and M56 are advised instead to take the M18 to York and then drive on to Scarborough or, indeed, to go to Edinburgh by train for a few days.

The food poisoning which reduced traffic to a crawl on the M3 on Saturday has now cleared and conditions are back to normal.

Experts have confirmed the reported discovery of oil along the M8, between Edinburgh and Glasgow, but it should be swept away by next weekend.

Parts of the M1 near Northampton were under water yesterday after a big brewery lorry shed its load.

The Old Spoon motorway service area will be closed on Wednesday and Thursday as it is being hired out for a private function (the national space invaders and pinball machine championships).

The building of a direct motorway link between Oxford and Cambridge has again been postponed indefinitely.

The National Motorway Gardens of Britain, which are situated on the banks of the M40 in the Chilterns, are now open to the public. They can be reached by leaving the M4 at Maidenhead and travelling cross-country via pretty lanes and muddy tracks.

Among the activities banned on motorways, with effect from this week, are hang-gliding, powered roller-skating, and the playing of musical instruments for gain, soliciting and canvassing for the Social Democrats. Frisbee-throwing from one side of the motorway to the other is allowed for a trial period.

The annual reunion of owners of repair garages along British motorways will take place this weekend in Honolulu and end sometime in April.

This year's production by the Motorway Staff Amateur Dramatic Society is a musical version of Jack Kerouac's *On the Road*. It opens on Saturday at Watford Gap, before going on to Newport Pagnell and all other service areas, and then a summer season in France.

The Arts Council is withdrawing its £10,000 grant for the maintenance of historical political graffiti on motorway bridges. 'If rude comments on the three-day week have survived until now,' an

Arts Council spokesman said, 'they are going to last a lot longer without our help.'

The controversial decision of the Government to hive off motorways to private ownership will be tested on Friday, with the public auctioning of the A41(M). Viewing is on Thursday, unless it is closed for repairs.

ALTHOUGH THE result of the Glasgow, Hillhead, by-election has not yet come in as I write these words—indeed, people have hardly started to vote—I think it is not too early to try to measure the impact of this extraordinary event.

Let us establish one thing straight from the start. Mr Jenkins's convincing victory/narrow defeat/humiliating trouncing has, if it has done nothing else, altered the face of British politics for all time/left things exactly as they were before/spelled out the death of the Social Democrats. Mr Jenkins is nothing if not a man of courage, and although there is a tendency in the Home Counties to see Glasgow as being 4,000 miles further away than it really is, it takes considerable personal bravery to volunteer to represent voters in another country, another class system and (sometimes, it seems) another language; as we now know this morning, Mr Jenkins's act was one of great perspicacity/more courage than sense/suicidal lunacy.

Of course, by-elections are often seen as totally media-created events/merely a chance for the public to express its dissatisfaction with the Government/a shining example of democracy in action, and so it has proved in this case. The thoughtful electors in this not untypical constituency on the banks of the River Clyde/Dee/Tay, have looked the issues fairly and squarely in the face and decided to vote according to their merits/write themselves into a footnote in history/spend all day in the pub as usual. It will be hard after this result ever to see the Labour Party as a credible opposition again/understand why we took the alliance seriously/doubt that Mrs Margaret Thatcher can fail to win the next election.

But one thing is certain/still unclear/worth churning out another column about. The result of this by-election spells out in the most unambitious way that we *must* introduce proportional representation immediately/build some better hotels in Hillhead/hold vital by-elections a bit closer to London. Nobody can deny that the SDP has now established itself as a new force in politics/just another party like the others/a dream that crumbled at the first touch of reality, and our political system simply has to be adapted so that it can reflect this in Parliament/keep Shirley Williams off the television/prevent those ludicrous midnight election results which so infuriate politicians/voters/me.

And what of Mr Jenkins's future? The way ahead now seems clear/drear/rosy/rosé/claret/hock/in pawn. All commentators agree that he has no option but to become the leader of the SDP/demand a recount/go and stand in the El Salvador elections. We may refer to him jokingly as Woy/Old Smoothie chops/the greatest politician since Disraeli/Asquith/Dick Taverne, but from today the humour must stop, for he has truly earned the right to national respect/final obscurity/a shooting squad and a last cigar.

Speaking personally, I can only take off my hat/take off in the next plane south from Glasgow. As I sit here surrounded by jubilant supporters/in a traffic jam on the M1/in a deserted *Times* building, I have only one message for Mr Jenkins and his merry crew of crusaders/carpet-baggers/middle-class idealists, and that is—Thank you! Thanks to you I now have faith in the future/ decided to emigrate/won £800 from my colleagues.

(This report appeared in some editions of yesterday's *Times*/last Monday's *Guardian*/Bernard Levin's book on the 1960s.)

'I'M JUST so thrilled!' said Maria Dallenhof last night, 'I never dreamt that I would ever receive an Oscar, and yet here I am! This has got to be the greatest night of my life! Wow! I don't know whether to laugh or cry!'

It was easy to understand Maria's emotion as she mingled with greats like Barry Norman who, until that moment, had just been names to her. She had been plucked from obscurity to go up on stage and receive the award for Best Supporting Actress to a Supporting Actress, which had been won by her best friend Debbie Hooch who was unable to appear. The way she had comported herself at the microphone, playing the part of the girl who doesn't know how to laugh or cry, had brought film offers flooding in as she left the stage—and this for a girl who has never acted in her life.

'My friend Debbie won this award for her part in *On Golden Pond*,' she said afterwards, half smiling, half sniffing. 'She plays the role of Jane Fonda's friend who looks after her in Paris. Unfortunately, it was all cut out of the final version that cinema

157

audiences have seen, but it's a stunning performance for all that and she deserves her Oscar terrifically.'

We in Britain do not perhaps appreciate just how really beautiful and wonderful it is for an American to get their hands on an Oscar (which stands, by the way, for Outstanding Screen Cinematograph Art Realization). Yesterday Maria was a topless hamburger waitress; tomorrow, as soon as she has sent on Debbie's award, she will be a star of the future. This could only happen in America.

'Can I just make two points?' she told us exclusively. 'One, it was the hamburgers that were topless—like, we didn't put buns on our 100 per cent prime beef. Two, this won't change my life. I've always behaved like a star.'

Debbie Hooch had to face fierce competition in the Best Supporting Actress to a Supporting Actress category from Linda Knowles, who played a patient who dies before the opening credits in *Whose Life Is It Anyway?*, Wendy Assher as the cousin of Lenin that we never see in *Reds*, and many others. How did Debbie feel when she heard about her Oscar (the initials, incidentally, stand for Opaline Statuette Chromed Against Rust)?

'Let's not talk about Debbie,' said Maria. 'I don't want to take anything away from her. Let's talk about me. And OK, yes, the waitresses were topless too, but it was all done in terrific taste. I think anyone who could carry off being a topless hamburger waitress would manage a big role in Hollywood with no trouble.'

Tomorrow Maria will be screen-tested for a possible role in a new film, *Topless Burger Bar II*, but today she can enjoy life as the girl who accepted an Oscar (Ornament Suitably Conspicuous And Revolting). And it was burgers on the house when she revisited her old haunt to show her colleagues the glittering trophy she had accepted in such a moving ceremony (Obligatory Speech Containing Abysmal Rhetoric).

Life will never be the same again for this erstwhile humble catering operative who has now joined the immortal ranks of those whom America honours as handlers of an Oscar (Organization of Socio-Cultural Artistic Riff-raff). Moreover. California.

By Appointment Satirist Royal

My Day
By Stanley Hoggis (who for 50 years has been the Royal Railway Porter-in-Waiting)

Many people seem to think that getting the Royal Family on to a train is easy. It isn't. They seem to think that once you're out of the State Coach you're somehow magically on the train. But you aren't. Somebody's got to get all that luggage from the Coach to the Royal Luggage Van. And that's me. The Royal Porter-in-Waiting. If you've ever wondered why royal parties seem to hang around on the platform a long time, shaking hands and telling the station master he's got a nice little station here, it's because they're waiting for me to get finished and give them the nod.

See, what happens is this. The State Coach arrives, and royalty get out, it might be one of them, it might be four or more. Then the Lord Chamberlain looks for a porter. Of course, he knows I'm there, lurking, but this is the tradition. 'Porter!' he cries. 'Porter! Oh, I say, there's no porter.' Then royalty says to him, 'What is the trouble, my Lord Chamberlain?' And he says, 'There is no porter to be had for love or money, your Majesty; there is never one when one wants one.'

This is all railway ritual, naturally, because then I come forward with the State Luggage Trolley and we have the following ceremonial exchange.

'Blimey, keep your hair on. What do you want taking?'

'All this luggage.'

'Whose luggage?'

'The Queen's luggage.'

'The Queen's moving house from the look of it. Stone the crows.'

I then fill up the State Trolley and take it to the Royal Luggage Van, and pretty soon it's all loaded up, assuming there's not too much mail or some blighter hasn't filled the van up with bicycles. After which we have another little ritual in which the Lord Chamberlain tips me, and it goes a bit like this.

'Here's a little tip.'

'You can say that again.'

'All right, make it a quid.'

Then I ceremonially give it back to him, and that's it, unless royalty has a complaint, like there's someone sitting in their reserved seat, which doesn't happen too often.

That's only on big days of course. Most days royalty isn't travelling so I'll spend it polishing the State Trolley. It's a big, ornate thing built for Edward VII, with separate lockers for whisky, playing cards, stuff like that. Or I'll go down to Victoria and practise being a porter, you know, grab a trolley marked 'For Passenger's

Use Only', keep tight hold of it and stand staring into the distance for hours on end. These days people are pretty tight with money and don't hire porters much—they just want to pick your brains about trains. I always tell them 'Platform 18', no matter what the question is. Never fails to work.

The present royalty are a good lot, but George VI was my favourite. I remember once he was going on an overnight trip to Carlisle, and by some mix-up I put all his luggage on the sleeper to Edinburgh. Next time he saw me he said, 'Hoggis, you acted like a real porter there,' and we had a good laugh. George VI was a very patient type and would have made a good railway porter himself, I think, but of course he had the misfortune to be born into the wrong social strata.

That's about it, really. Oh, thank you, squire. No, really, that's fine, if that's all you can afford.

(Stanley Hoggis was talking to Miles Kington.)